AF454295

The Russian Catastrophe

and Chances to Overcome It

MUNI
PRESS

Andrey Borisovich Zubov

The Russian Catastrophe

and Chances to Overcome It

MASARYK UNIVERSITY PRESS

ISBN 978-80-280-0384-5
ISBN 978-80-280-0385-2 (online ; pdf)
https://doi.org/10.5817/CZ.MUNI.M280-0385-2023

Table of Contents

Introduction

Professor Zubov at Masaryk University

It is a great honour for me to give a brief introduction to this book by Professor Andrey Borisovich Zubov, who was born in Moscow in 1952. This prominent figure in contemporary Russian historiography, religious studies and political science enjoys an exceptional relationship with our university. Following the Russian occupation of Crimea in 2014, which Professor Zubov strongly criticized, Mikuláš Bek, the predecessor to our present rector Martin Bareš, offered him a teaching post at Masaryk University. At that point, however, the Russian scholar did not take up the offer. Although he expressed his deepest gratitude, he stated he would prioritize remaining in Russia for as long as possible and working on behalf of the liberal opposition there, which he did indeed do despite immense personal difficulty. He had to leave his university, the Moscow State Institute of International Relations, where he had held a prominent position, and he was stripped of all his other posts for disagreeing with the policies of the Russian Federation. For the enlightened reader this story provides more than one parallel with the experiences of the Czech writers and academics who were placed under significant pressure during the period of Normalization and often had to choose between the risks of staying in their country and emigration.

A milestone in the relationship between Professor Zubov and Masaryk University was reached in 2019 when the university decided to honour this courageous academic with the title of Doctor honoris causa, the highest award which can be conferred by a public university in the Czech Republic. In the laudation given by the then deputy rector Petr Dvořák at the presentation of the honorary doctorate, emphasis was placed not only on the academic work of the nominee in the field of history, but also on his interdisciplinary activities and in particular his original and critical approach towards post-1991 Russian history, which culminated in editing a towering work entitled A History of 20th Century Russia (incidentally, this book was published in two volumes in Czech by Argo publishers though it has yet to be translated into English). The laureate then took the opportunity in his address to analyse the situation in Russian today within the context of the turbulent, painful history of the 19th and 20th centuries; he reminded us of Masaryk's project to help refugees from Russia after the Bolshevik revolution of 1917; and he expressed his profound commitment to democracy and respect for human rights.

From today's perspective his remarks concerning developments in other countries were also prescient: "Some of those 12 countries (of the former USSR) are now making strenuous efforts to free themselves from their communist past and turn towards Europe... These include Georgia, Ukraine, Armenia and Moldavia. Others have become paralyzed within a new totalitarianism, sometimes even harsher than during the Soviet era, such as in Turkmenistan and Uzbekistan. Meanwhile, Slavic Russia and Belarus have mostly travelled the sad road from building a market democracy back to authoritarian despotism, where there is no protection of human life, property or political and civil rights... How to overcome this regression in freedom, how can Russia and Belarus, who are suffering under authoritarianism, return to Europe? How to help Ukraine transform from an oligarchical, semi-anarchistic country into a truly democratic and legal state?"

To a certain extent these questions were answered by the events of February 2022, when the Russian Federation attacked Ukraine and ignited a conflict which has accelerated the aforementioned processes. Russia and Belarus have adopted ever more authoritarian methods of government and have thus isolated themselves from the democratic world, while the embattled Ukrainians have turned towards a more Western understanding of the state and global and European structures (the EU and NATO). However, the beginning of Russia's unsuccessful invasion not only meant a sea change in European political thinking (for example, a few years ago who could have imagined Finland being a member of NATO with Sweden next in line to join this military alliance!), but also personal changes for Andrey Borisovich Zubov. That year he was also suddenly confronted with the idea of having to leave Russia, as staying in his homeland, where he was a fierce critic of Vladimir Putin, was becoming increasingly dangerous. Professor Zubov finally came to a decision. Following the announcement of partial mobilization in September 2022, he decided to leave his homeland. He would later justify this decision by stating that if he had remained, two paths would have been left open to him: silence or imprisonment. He refused to be silenced and so shortly before the closure of the Finnish border, under quite dramatic circumstances he crossed the border in his own car, travelling halfway across Europe to Brno, where Masaryk University offered him asylum and a position as guest lecturer.

Professor Zubov has been a member of the academic community of our university since the autumn semester of 2022, and in addition to his regular teaching he also participates in a large number of debates and discussions. Brno has also provided him with a kind of base from which he can also travel abroad – i.e., to places where he can freely work, lecture, and explain his ideas and standpoints. In connection to this I would like to mention that in order for Professor Zubov to feel at home in Brno and Masaryk University, the management of the Faculty of Arts and the staff at the Centre of International Cooperation have been of great assistance. Without their help it would have been impossible to overcome many of the obstacles which stood in the way of fully integrating this Russian professor into our academic community.

I was personally moved by what Professor Zubov wrote for the university's Magazine M after his arrival: "Although in recent years I had been trying to offer private lessons in Russia, what truly fulfils me is lecturing freely to students. I am therefore immensely grateful to Masaryk University that I can now once more be in contact with students on academic soil."

The university community now has its disposal an edited version of the lectures he gave at Masaryk University's Faculty of Arts shortly after his arrival in the Czech Republic and Brno in the autumn semester of 2022. There was an unforgettable atmosphere at these lectures as they attracted people from both academia and the general public. It is also worth pointing out that Professor Zubov was under intense media scrutiny. These lectures were also unique because the professor could now openly discuss developments in his country and the destructive policies of its leadership – of course, as is his custom, he would incorporate the situation today within the deeper layers of history and historical memory.

I would like to stress how difficult it is for any academic to lecture on the history of their own country at a time when that country has gone to war with its neighbour, a war which not only threatens Ukraine but peace for the whole of Europe. Moreover, Professor Zubov's lectures are being given in a university which has hundreds of young students as well as teachers from Ukraine. And it is pleasing to note that Professor Zubov's qualities are demonstrated not only in his discussions with Czechs but also with his Ukrainian colleagues.

Following consultations with the author, Masaryk University Press decided to bring out this book in English. The reasoning was not only because the lectures were originally given in English but also because the text and the ideas which it contains could therefore be disseminated abroad, which is important for both Professor Zubov and for the development of Russian as well as European democratic structures. This book might even reach the democratically minded intelligentsia within Russia itself.

Jiří Hanuš
vice-rector of Masaryk University
28 September 2023

About my lectures

On March 1, 2014, as Putin was preparing to annex Crimea, the website of the daily newspaper Vedomosti published my column entitled 'We've seen it before'[1]. The reaction was immediate. I was quickly expelled from the Moscow State Institute of International Relations (MGIMO University), the very institution from which I had graduated long ago in 1973 and where I had been a professor of philosophy and religious studies since 2001. After my resignation, I received messages of support and offers of collaboration from many universities and academic centres around the world, but not from Russia. From that moment on, all formal possibilities for research or teaching in my home country were closed to me. I wasn't surprised, I knew what I was doing.

One of the first letters came from Mikuláš Bek, then Rector of Masaryk University in Brno. Dr Bek proposed me a professorship at this famous Czech University and invited me to continue my academic career there. I thanked him but refused, as I had done with other similar offers. I believed that even if I was deprived of the right to carry out my work in Russia, I should stay in the country to help it overcome the growing authoritarianism of Putin's regime and find the path to democracy and peaceful coexistence with all nations. To this end, I changed my rule of staying out of politics and decided to run in the 2016 parliamentary elections. After an expected defeat, I joined the People's Freedom Party (PARNAS), of which I am still vice-president.

The invitations to leave the country and teach in the 'free world' kept coming. But it was not until 2022, when Russia launched a full-scale war of aggression against Ukraine and Putin's authoritarian regime was unmistakeably evolving into a totalitarian dictatorship, that with a heavy heart I made the difficult decision to accept. Although I was very reluctant to go abroad, it was becoming increasingly dangerous to stay in Moscow. Many of my friends and colleagues had already been silenced, and some had

---

1 Андрей Зубов, „Это уже было," Ведомости (March 2014). Available at https://www.vedomosti.ru/opinion/articles/2014/03/01/andrej-zubov-eto-uzhe-bylo

been imprisoned. My fate would probably have been the same. So I accepted with gratitude the invitation of Dr Martin Bareš, the new rector of Masaryk University.

I was asked to give a series of lectures on Russian history, which I did, uniting them under the general title of the 'Reasons for the Russian Catastrophe of the 20th Century and Possibilities To Overcome It'. I believed then, as I do now, that it is an essential topic to study in order to try to answer two closely related questions:

1. Why in the twentieth century, after the Bolshevik coup, Russia has been a constant source of aggression, from the attempted conquest of Ukraine and Finland in January and February 1918, to the brutal war against Ukraine, which began in February 2014 and has been going on ever since, taking a more heinous form every day?
2. Is there any hope that Russia can change radically, stop being an aggressor and become a peace-loving democratic nation like the EU and NATO countries? And if there is (I'm sure there is), what should Russia and the world do to make this vision a reality?

I tried to suggest my answers in the six lectures I gave in Brno between October and November 2022 in English. The university later proposed to publish them as a short book. I agreed with enthusiasm, hoping that my texts would contribute to a better understanding of the processes that led to the war, and thus to the building of a more lasting peace once it is over.

Putin's bloodthirsty regime, which unleashed the war, should undoubtedly find itself in the dock of an international tribunal. But Russia, as a nation won't vanish, just as other nations that committed atrocities in the past – France, Germany, Austria, Turkey, Japan, Italy, etc. – didn't disappear from the map. In all previous cases, the peoples responsible for the aggressions have repented and, together with the world community, have found new, often painful and uncertain, but very reliable ways to a peaceful and dignified life.

I am sure that the Russian people are also capable of finding a path that will lead our country into a future where Russia will no longer be associated with aggression, perfidy, cruelty, lies, murder and insatiable thirst for domination over its neighbours, but will become a stronghold of democracy, economic prosperity and international peace, much like present-day Japan, Italy, Germany and France. I earnestly hope that the compilation of my lectures delivered in Brno, will contribute to this much desired purpose.

I would like to take this pleasant opportunity to express my sincere gratitude to those without whom these lectures and this book would not have been possible: Mikuláš Bek, the current Minister of Education of the Czech Republic, Martin Bareš, Rector of Masaryk University, Jiří Hanuš, Vice-Rector, and Irena Radová, Dean of the Faculty of Philosophy, who helped me to organize my academic work in Brno and made the publication of this book possible.

My English is far from perfect. In speech, emotions can help avoid ambiguity, but in writing, mistakes cannot be hidden. I would never have dared to present these lectures to you, dear readers, without the assistance of my friends Chris Rance, an English teacher at Masaryk University, and Anton Klevansky, a conference interpreter and translator.

Many will find these texts too superficial, full of common knowledge, others may view them as politically biased. I take full responsibility for any of their flaws. I have done what I could, and if my work contributes in any way to a better understanding of the tragic fate of my people in past and present centuries, I will consider my mission accomplished.

Andrey Zubov
Brno. July 2023

The enigma of Russia

Dear colleagues, I thank all those who invited me to Masaryk University in Brno during these turbulent times for my country. Not only has this invitation allowed me to continue my work when doing so in Moscow would be nearly impossible, but it also provides me with a platform to share the truth about Russia with the wider world.

This truth is especially important here in Czechia, where the people have traditionally entertained amicable relations with the Russians. As a result, many were caught off guard by the appalling actions of Putin's government in Ukraine and elsewhere. I hope that this new cycle of lectures will shed light on the realities of modern-day Russia.

Over the next six weeks, I will be giving a new lecture every Wednesday evening. My goal is to examine the reasons behind the Russian catastrophe of the last century and consider how its consequences can be addressed in the 21st century. I'm sure that the 20th century in Russia did not end with the collapse of the Soviet Union or even with the reforms of Perestroika. In some way or another, the country continues to be mired in its past.

My first lecture, titled 'The Enigma of Russia', delves into the question of what Russia truly is. For many foreigners, my homeland remains a riddle and an enigma. But what is Russia after all?

Between 1991 and 2022, Russia projected an image of a normal Western country, and quite a few nations around the world still prefer to hold on to this view, treating Russia as a typical albeit very large European state. It wasn't until the horrific events of February 24 that attitudes among democracies began to shift. People throughout Europe, North America, and the democratic states of the Asia-Pacific region, including Japan, South Korea, the Republic of China (Taiwan), Singapore, Australia, and New Zealand, were taken aback.

Russia had revealed itself to be a completely different country, drastically at odds with the image that had been maintained for decades. This realization has led to a re-evaluation of how democratic nations should approach Russia in the future.

I vividly recall the aftermath of the collapse of the Soviet Union in December 1991, when Francis Fukuyama, a prominent American philosopher and thinker of Hegelian school, published an article and a book titled 'The End of History'.[2] Fukuyama argued that history, as a struggle between good and evil, had ended, and that liberal democracy and human rights would henceforth prevail. Only in a few remote regions of the Third World would human relations and international affairs continue to be irrational and devoid of justice.

At that time, I was forty years old, about the same age as Dr Fukuyama, and I wrote an article, explaining that his view was misguided. While Hegel's understanding of history is beautiful, it is too naive and fails to take into account human nature. I argued that the worst was yet to come, and that we would have to confront it soon. To be honest, I didn't believe that the worst would come from Russia. Like the majority of my educated compatriots, I hoped that the era of totalitarianism and communism had passed, and that the only thing we still had to figure out was how to build a new Russia.[3]

We were faced with a difficult question: how should we proceed? We didn't fully comprehend the nature and origins of Western democracy, or the workings of modern European and First World economies. Even experts in the field had only a vague understanding of these matters. As a result, we made many mistakes, but that is not the focus of my lecture. My topic is rather why Russia chose to take the path of aggression and despotism, destroying democracy and violating civil rights.

Fukuyama, among other scholars, believed that there was no turning back from democracy and liberalism towards a totalitarian past. Yet, it did happen, and therefore this possibility is clearly present. Under the leadership of President Putin, Russia has taken this disastrous path.

Many Europeans tend to overlook the differences between the development of Russia and other post-communist countries in Eastern and Central Europe. They often assume that Poland, the Czech Republic, Estonia, or Lithuania went through the same processes as Russia, but this wasn't the case. The paths taken were different, and the results we see now differ as well. It was only after Putin's infamous speech in Munich on February 10, 2007, that a small group of more conscious and sagacious politicians finally realized that something was amiss, that the Russian president's words were in stark contrast to acceptable political behaviour in the post-war Europe. Only those on the far right of the European political spectrum, like Marine Le Pen, did not shy away from using the same language.

Unhindered, Putin sprang into action, and his actions spoke even louder than his words. In August 2008, Russia resorted to violence on its borders for the first time,

---

2   Francis Fukuyama, *The End of History and the Last Man* (New York: Free Press, 1992). See also his "The End of History?", *The National Interest*, no. 16 (Summer 1989).

3   Европа и мир: Рубежи земли и предназначение цивилизаций // Континент (Москва-Paris). 1995, № 83.— С.249 -270.

against Georgia, and occupied South Ossetia and Abkhazia. While there were some ethnic tensions between the Georgian population, the Abkhazians, and the Ossetians, they should have been resolved without military force, with the assistance of the European structures, perhaps involving the OSCE or the EU. Nothing of the sort happened. Russia captured these territories and established military bases there. Europe was shocked but once again decided to let it be, hoping that Putin would stop. It was a terrible mistake. Six years later, at the beginning of 2014, Putin took another step. He annexed Crimea and started a war in eastern Ukraine.

Europe finally began to take this change of direction seriously and sanctions were imposed on Moscow. Russia was expelled from the G7, and contacts with NATO were put on hold. Nevertheless, despite these measures, relations between Russia and the West remained largely unchanged. It wasn't until February 24, 2022, that Europe's attitude towards Russia underwent a complete reversal. Today, the sight of Ukrainian flags and symbols across Europe is a powerful reminder that this continent has finally taken sides and joined forces with Ukraine against Putin's aggression.

Why was Russia's turnabout possible and how did it happen? How could an authoritarian regime take power after thirty years of democracy, albeit a strange one? How did we fail to recognize the change in Putin's intentions? Those are complex questions that require in-depth discussion.

Let's start by analysing some common explanations. Some argue that *Russia has always been predisposed to totalitarian rule*, that it has always been a totalitarian state, governed by a succession of authoritarian leaders, sometimes with short intervals between them. Others attribute it to *genetics*, claiming that the Russians possess an inclination towards savagery, cruelty, and imperialism due to a unique genetic make-up. The third possible answer is that *Russia is an Asian country*, geographically part of Europe, but culturally and mentally closer to Asia. Apparently, this should explain why a human life is worth almost nothing there and human rights are often despised. Yet, I think all three of these answers are wrong.

Let's start with the first one. It is based on a certain philosophical worldview, so it is important to explain why it is conceptually flawed. Absolute predisposition does not exist in the human world. While we may speak of certain inclinations, every individual and every nation possess the free will to choose between good and evil, to either ruin the world or rebuild it. And everyone has a moral obligation to resist negative impulses. Therefore, any explanation that relies on some natural predisposition to evil is fundamentally flawed. Every human being and every civilization are free in their choices and actions.

The case of Germany is rather well known. In 1933, the Germans voted for the Nazis and supported them until the end of World War II. However, deliberate systematic denazification efforts after the war transformed their mindset and paved the way for a free and democratic German state today. It is a convincing proof that people can change themselves by the power of their free will and turn from evil to good. Germany is not an isolated case, as Japan and many other countries offer additional examples.

Now *let's turn our attention to another set of answers that brings up the topic of a social genotype*. I do not believe that such a thing exists at all. Genes are a biological reality and not a social phenomenon. A genotype is necessarily linked to an individual, and any genetic error may lead to personal health issues but cannot determine the fate of an entire nation. Therefore, any mention of bad and good genes in a social, political, or historical context is senseless. Furthermore, even metaphorical use should be discouraged, as social genotyping leads to racism. Similar talk about national supremacy was widespread in the 18th, 19th, and even the beginning of the 20th century (think about the Nazis). Reviving it would be an unacceptable mistake.

The same arguments hold true if we try to react to the *third explanation above, the one referring to Asian mentality*. Asia is not necessarily a region of despotism. Japan, South Korea, Taiwan, Singapore, India, and even Sri Lanka in many regards are normal democratic countries.

Speaking of civilizations, it's impossible to overlook the seminal work of Arnold J. Toynbee. In his *Study of History*, he singles out the Russian civilization as a part of a larger European civilization. Toynbee's starting point was the Minoan (or Cretan) civilization of the third and second millennia BC. By the end of the second millennium, it split into two mighty branches: Roman and Hellenic. It was from the Hellenic civilization that the medieval Byzantine civilization evolved, which spread across the Orthodox states of the Balkans and the Christian states of the Caucasus. The Byzantine civilization gave birth among others to the Russian civilization, which still exists today. On the other hand, the Roman civilization gave rise to the medieval European civilization and to the unique Far Western Civilization of the Celts of the British Isles, which later faded away. Therefore, we can rightly consider the Russian civilization to be a first or second cousin of the modern Western European civilization, both resting on the same ancient foundation. They also interacted strongly in different historical periods. Therefore, Russia belongs to the family of European civilizations, as also evidenced by its language and history[4].

It can be concluded that there are no intrinsic reasons for the Russian catastrophe of the 20th century. We must therefore study the historical causes that led to it. It is clear that Russia's conduct today differs from that of most European states, and we have to understand why. To find an explanation, we need to make a synchronic comparison between historical processes in Russia and those in other European societies.

For this purpose, it's not necessary to delve too deeply into Russian history, which spans some 1100 years. I'll start from Muscovy state, i.e. from the fifteenth century. This is when the historical trajectories of Russia and Western Europe started to diverge.

---

4   Arnold J. Toynbee, *A Study of History* (London: Oxford University Press, 1987).

In Europe it was the time of the Renaissance, a period marked by a concerted effort to reconnect with the ancient Greco-Roman world and its pre-Christian culture. Classical texts were revived and became required reading for anyone considered educated. Search for historical roots was a defining feature of that time.

The consequences of this search can be seen in the works of fine art, literature, fiction, and theatre. Shakespeare's dramas, for example, drew heavily from ancient Greek tragedy and the writings of Seneca. The revival of ancient sources during the Renaissance was so significant that it is impossible to imagine modern Europe without it.

The situation in Russia was dramatically different. Prior to the mid-15th century, it had been part of the Byzantine world, Byzantine Commonwealth as Prince Dimitri Obolensky, Russian emigrant historian, used to call it[5]. The link with the ancient tradition in Byzantine culture was never broken, as there had been no equivalent to the European Dark Ages in Constantinople.

The Byzantine tradition was kept alive in Russia through ancient texts that flowed from Byzantium, sometimes written in the Old Slavonic language. In the mid-15th century, however, the flow of knowledge was abruptly cut off, as if a wall had risen between Constantinople and Moscow. Interestingly, this occurred at the same time that the medieval wall between Europe and the ancient world was being demolished. It's also important to note that these events only affected the Muscovite State and not Kyivan Rus, the region that eventually became Ukraine and never lost its connection to Byzantium and the West.

The disruption began with the conclusions of the Councils of Ferrara and Florence in Italy in 1439, which proclaimed a union between the Catholic and the Byzantine worlds. This union was never accepted by Moscow. A few years later, Constantinople was taken by the Ottomans, which was seen in Russia as a punishment for this attempted union with Rome.

It was believed in Russia that the preservation of pure orthodoxy was their duty and the only right path. As the monk Filofei (Philotheus) of Pskov, one of the leading ecclesiastical authorities of that time, wrote in his letters to Vasily III, *Russian tsar was the only guardian of the real Orthodox faith.* Therefore, Muscovite Church sought autonomy from 'corrupt' Constantinople and declared autocephaly in 1448. But independence brought its development to an abrupt halt, it was unable to thrive without drawing upon the great ancient Christian and pre-Christian traditions of Rome and Byzantium.

It was the end of a long and beautiful cultural collaboration. In the early years of the 16th century with the death of Dionisius, an outstanding icon painter who rivalled Giotto in his mastery, great tradition of wonderful Russian painting came to an end. The spiritual movement of non-possessors (*nestyazhateli*), inspired by the Byzantines, disappeared. These were monks, initially centred around the monastery of Saint Sergius near Moscow, who deliberately renounced all possessions and devoted their lives

---

5   Dimitri Obolensky, *The Byzantine Commonwealth: Eastern Europe, 500-1453* (London: Cardinal, 1971).

to spiritual ideals, following Christ's teachings in search of personal salvation. Their communities were destroyed during the reign of Ivan IV the Terrible.

While Europe and even Kyiv were witnessing the revival of links with the world of antiquity, Muscovy went in the opposite direction, completely renouncing the continuity of this tradition in the middle of the 15th century.

Later, in the 16th century, Russia copied some European practices – but what kind of practices! It was an era of despotic rulers in many parts of Europe, a phenomenon that Machiavelli both described and perhaps even contributed to. These leaders were focused solely on maintaining power at all costs, disregarding any spiritual or moral principles. Figures such as Henry VIII of England, Cosimo Medici of Tuscany and Ivan IV the Terrible of Russia were all emblematic of this new type of ruler. While their similarities are striking, the societies they ruled were vastly different.

European societies during the 15th and 16th centuries were profoundly influenced by the Reformation movement. Whatever reservations one might have, it was a positive phenomenon primarily because of its emphasis on the use of national languages. Luther's translation of the Bible into German is widely believed to be the beginning of the modern German. Shortly thereafter, King James commissioned an English translation, and many countries, including those in the Baltic region, followed suit. This was a significant moment as common people began to read and discuss biblical texts with their families and friends, questioning their own beliefs and reflecting on humanistic and moral ideas. Christian moral principles became firmly embedded in their consciousness. In Europe, the Protestant evangelical tradition and the Catholic faith had been at odds since the 16th century, yet they have also deeply influenced each other. This is especially true here in Moravia, where Protestants (Lutherans, Calvinists, Hussites) and Catholics have lived side by side for centuries. For all of them, personal moral principles have become fundamental. It is no coincidence that the Moravian Brethren movement emerged not far from here, in Herrnhut, at the beginning of the 18th century. This movement placed particular emphasis on Bible study, personal faith, and moral values.

Nothing like that occurred in Russia. Bible was written in Slavonic, old Bulgarian language, that was not easily understood by native Russian speakers. Failure to understand the sacred texts doesn't help to absorb their philosophical and moral concepts. Illiteracy was so widespread among the population that even some priests were unable to read the scripture. Unlike in Europe, there was no mutual exchange and cross-fertilization of ideas between Catholics, Lutherans, and Calvinists. Consequently, the majority of people did not have their own personal moral values and judgments.

The invention of the printing press by Gutenberg was another major factor that contributed to the divergence between Western Europe and Russia. The widespread availability of printed books led to an increase in literacy in the West, particularly among evangelical communities. In contrast, printing in Russia was limited to ecclesiastical purposes, and did little to improve general education. In fact, in the 15th and 16th centuries, there was a sharp decline in literacy levels, which was in stark contrast to the previous century when a significant portion of the population in Novgorod knew how to read and write. This is evident from the many personal letters on birch bark (*beresta*) that have survived to this day.

It is evident that the differences above are not due to any biological anomaly, but rather stem from the deliberate choice made by the Russian people acting in their own free will, to seek autocephaly for their church and to distance themselves from Rome. Although even then, some individuals and spiritual leaders thought it was an unwise move, the decision was taken, and we are still reaping its bitter fruits.

An additional point worth noting is the peculiar land ownership system that emerged in Russia. Unlike in Europe, there were only two forms of land ownership: princes' estates and possessions of small landowners. Mongol invasion prompted many people from the south to flee to the north-east, seeking refuge from the nomadic tribes. Local landowners granted them land on conditional tenure. The only regions where small private properties still dominated were in the extreme north (Novgorod Republic) or north-west (Pskov Republic), and in Belarusian territories around Polotsk and Minsk.

As a large proportion of the nobility were exterminated during the reign of Ivan IV the Terrible, their possessions were taken over by the state. This explains why after the Time of Troubles (at the beginning of the 17th century), only a relatively small portion of land remained in the hands of the nobility, and even less in the north was owned by peasants. The largest share of arable land belonged to the Church and to the State. Consequently, *the population in general lost the habit of owning private property*. Responsible property ownership was quite rare among the peasants, who made up the vast majority of the Russian population at the time.

At the beginning of the 17th century a new dynasty, the Romanovs, came to power. It was a time when Russia tried to adopt the European methods of organizing its society. The tsar ruled with the help of the Parliament (*Duma*), and the Holy Council (*Osvyashchenny Sobor*), which brought together the patriarch, bishops, and heads of monasteries. The Duma's role was to propose laws for the tsar to approve. Similar and perhaps even less democratic forms of land councils existed at that time in France and nearly the same in England.

In 1649 a special session of the parliament passed a new code of laws introducing a new social concept called *tyaglo* or 'burden'. According to this principle, everyone in the country, including the tsar, monks, priests, bishops, peasants, and soldiers, had their own *tyaglo*. The tsar's 'burden' was to rule the state, while the nobility was supposed to defend it. The clergy's 'burden' was to pray for it, and the peasants had to work for it and, during times of war, to fight for it.

Russia was not a wealthy country, and its treasury often ran out of money. So, when the tsar needed to pay someone for their work or service, he would often compensate them in kind, by giving them a village, along with its inhabitants who had to pay part of their income as tribute to their new lord and the remainder to the state. State peasants were required to pay all their taxes to the state in kind and occasionally, in cash. This system allowed individuals to retain their personal freedom, but they were no longer independent in their work. They had to stay in their villages and work not only for themselves but also for their landlords or the state. Even the nobility had no right to change their place of residence without prior authorization.

Similar arrangements were not uncommon in other parts of Europe at the time. Their popularity in Russia can be attributed to the vast size of the country and the inability of the state to collect taxes directly in such sparsely populated areas. This form of social relations was not efficient as it favoured non-monetary exchanges, which failed to create the necessary dynamics for the country's economic development. To address this issue, Russian Tsars were looking for potential solutions.

In the mid-17th century, Tsar Alexis (*Alexei Mikhailovich*) thought it was time to rebuild relations with the Orthodox world, beginning with Constantinople. His decision was prompted by a political opportunity: in 1648, the Cossacks in Ukraine rebelled and sought reunification with Muscovy, which eventually led to the signing of an agreement in Pereyaslav on the Dnipro in 1654. This agreement made the left bank of Ukraine an autonomous part of the Russian tsardom. Given the close connections between the Ukrainian Orthodox Church and Constantinople, Tsar Alexis sought to leverage this situation in order to bring his state closer to the world Orthodox patriarchates.

In 1666–1667, a Church Council was held in Moscow, attended by three patriarchs and many bishops from the lands of the former Byzantine Empire. They adopted a declaration acknowledging that previous decisions claiming the autonomy and spiritual distinctiveness of the Russian church were wrong, 'whispered by the winds in their heads' as the authors of the document put it. Instead, they recognized the need for the Russian Church to be reintegrated into the world Orthodoxy.

In history and politics, however, it is often as challenging to bring down a wall as it is to build one. Over the course of fifteen decades of self-proclaimed autocephaly and hostility towards Catholics and Lutherans, several generations of Russian people grew accustomed to the idea that their church was special. So, when the Church Council declared in 1667 that this unique Russian way was a 'mistake of the mind', many Russians disagreed, and the Old Believers (*staroobryadtsy*) movement was born.

The Old Believers went so far as to proclaim the Tsar the Antichrist and the official Church the Church of Satan. In an effort to protect their ideas, they sought separation from Russian society. From a doctrinal standpoint, they were wrong, but they were sincere, if sometimes naive, in their piety, and generally very good Christians. Tragically, more than 20,000 of them were executed by the State or committed suicide to avoid falling into the hands of the tsar's administration. As a result, Russian society lost a large group of devout Christians in the last third of the 17th century. The tradition of Old Believers is still alive today.

The children of tsar Alexis contributed significantly to further reintegration of Russia into European and world civilization. His son, Fyodor (1676–1682), and his daughter, Sophia (1682–1689), who succeeded each other on the throne, decided to abandon the *tyaglo* principle and adopt the most advanced system of the time – private land ownership and taxation. Their plan was to give land to peasants as private property, collect taxes from them, and use the revenue to fund the army and the state bureaucracy. These were standard, modern principles of economic organization at that time.

Fyodor and Sophia tried to emulate Poland's reforms, but they realized that a country like Russia, with poor soil and limited resources, could not modernize its economy and wage war at the same time. Therefore, they rushed to establish an 'eternal peace' with Poland. Under the terms of the peace treaty signed in 1686, Russia gained control of Kyiv. Many historians consider this period to be the best years for ordinary Russians. They felt themselves to be free and were generally quite prosperous.

But any significant, lasting change takes time, and the next tsar, Peter the Great, who was the half-brother of Fyodor and Sophia (they had different mothers), was unwilling to wait. Instead, he decided to transform everything at once and become a European without any preparation and without any economic rationale. His approach was completely different from that of his predecessors. Rather than trying to help people become wealthy and enrich the state through their taxes, Peter wanted to build a large army and navy here and now. To achieve this, he was prepared to extract as much money as possible from the population, without any regard to their welfare. His goal was not to match Europe in prosperity. He wanted to rival Europe in military strength.

Peter's reforms were terrible in their brutal simplicity. The entire population, from peasants to nobles, was subjected to a form of servitude. All land was declared to be state property, and all citizens were obliged to work for the state. The principle of *tyaglo* was reintroduced and applied universally. The peasants lost their land and personal autonomy, and all their property became the possession of the nobility, whose property in turn belonged to the tsar.

Despite living vastly different lifestyles, with the nobility embracing a Westernized way of life actively enforced by Peter, and the impoverished and traditionalist peasants, both groups were ultimately enslaved by the tsar. This oppressive system is known as serfdom, and the peasants were referred to as *serfs*. Their fate was indeed similar to that of the ancient Roman *servi* (i.e. slaves).

It is fair to say that in the early 18th century, Peter the Great reintroduced slavery to Russia. Peasants were stripped of their land, property, and livestock, and could be sold at the whim of their landlord. It was not uncommon for spouses to be sold separately or for children to be taken from their parents. Landlords could cede their peasants, with or without land, to anyone they saw fit, with the approval of the authorities. All land was technically owned by the state, but this changed with the introduction of a new law on February 18, 1762, under Emperor Peter III, which allowed private ownership of land by the nobility.

According to the renowned Russian historian Vasily Klyuchevsky, Peter III should have announced a law the following day that would have granted land ownership rights to the peasants as well. This never happened, however, and the peasants had to wait another 99 years before serfdom was finally abolished on February 19, 1861. For almost 150 years, beginning with Peter's reforms of 1703 and 1711, the overwhelming majority of the Russian population (peasants made up 92%-95% thereof) were deprived of the right to own property. This had a profound impact on Russian mentality.

The Austrian monarchy, like Russia, also went through a period of absolutist rule, but it was different in two important ways. Firstly, ordinary people were allowed to own property, and this right was respected. No confiscation without a court order was allowed. Secondly, the absolutist rulers of the Austrian Empire and Prussia *governed without the people but for the people.* The rulers' duty was to improve the lives of their subjects and to increase their income, without depriving them of their civil rights. In pursuit of these goals, European monarchs sought to increase literacy rates and even introduced local self-government. While there were many positive changes in central Europe during the 18th century, the situation in Russia was very different. The tsar continued to rule *without the people, for himself and a small group of nobles.*

Russia became a state that primarily served the aristocracy rather than the common people, which often led to conflicts of interest between the two groups. As a result, Russian history is marked by numerous instances of turmoil and unrest, including the Pugachev's Rebellion of 1773–1775.

Russian rulers were not interested in educating common people, especially the peasants, who were kept completely illiterate. Even church services were incomprehensible to them, as they were conducted in Old Slavonic. Although peasants attended religious ceremonies, they were unable to grasp the meaning of more than a few words in the chants. As a result, despite being sincerely religious they lacked a deep understanding of their faith.

In contrast, the Old Believers made great efforts to learn and understand Old Slavonic, and even tried to read books. Within their communities, a concept called *nachetniki* emerged, which referred to those who could read not only for themselves but also for a group of fellow believers.

When the Great Reforms began in Russia in February 1861 with the accession to the throne of Alexander II, most ordinary people were illiterate, had no property and no access to medical care. This was the result of poor governance and misguided policies of the previous leaders. While there were exceptions, such as Sophia and Fyodor, other rulers had their own agenda which didn't really take into account people's interests.

Nevertheless, in conclusion, I would like to note that while the situation in Russia was undoubtedly difficult and complex, it was not necessarily unique compared to other European countries. For example, serfdom was abolished in Austria in 1781, eighty years before Russia. In Prussia, where it was particularly terrible in Slavic lands, it was outlawed by Baron Heinrich von Stein in 1807, and in Hungary, Emperor Franz Joseph put an end to serfdom in 1848.

The Slavery Abolition Act was passed in the British Empire in 1833. It was gradually implemented until August 1, 1838, when it was finally enforced in Jamaica and other Caribbean islands. And, of course, slavery was abolished in the United States in 1865, four years after Russia. So, the timing in Russia was not particularly bad, although the level of education of the general population was lower than that of British and American slaves.

Also, in March 1803 already, Emperor Alexander I granted non-nobles the right to own agricultural land as private property. Merchants and the clergy were able to exercise this right, as were some peasants who were finally able to buy their freedom.

Russia's Great Reforms of the 1860s largely mirrored the path taken by most European states in the first half of the century. There were some differences, but not fundamental ones. Many countries on other continents were also inspired by European liberalism, such as Japan (Meiji reforms) or the Ottoman Empire (Tanzimat reforms). In the 18th century already, several countries attempted to emulate republican France, and later England and the United States became models for much of the world. Russia may have chosen to follow the example of other European nations, but ultimately took a different path.

Liberation of Russia

In my first lecture, I spoke about the Russian Empire, which is often referred to as a 'society of serfs'. I argued, however, that because of total suppression of freedoms, a more accurate description would be a 'society of slaves'.

Russian serfdom was essentially a form of slavery and posed a major challenge to society. Absolutist rule in Russia, unlike in Austria, Prussia, or France, had two distinct features that would have a lasting impact on the country's future. First, serfdom was not just a form of coercion; for the peasants it did mean *total enslavement*. Landlord had the power to buy and sell not only their land but also individuals. It went as far as buying and selling peasants without land, breaking families (selling spouses separately or taking children away from their parents) and even controlling marriages. The entire population was thus in a state of absolute personal subjugation.

The second crucial difference was that serfs, the majority of the population at that time, had no private property whatsoever. They were not allowed to own land, cattle, houses, or anything else. Landlords had the power to use any of their peasants' possessions for their own benefit without constraint. Moreover, serfs had no right to take legal action against their masters. The landlord was the ultimate authority in all matters, and even if a peasant dared to lodge an official complaint with the tsar or the governor, the law would usually punish the complainant himself rather than the offender. Punishments could include exile to Siberia or other severe penalties.

Russian society was not free at all. And the beneficiaries of this state of affairs were the nobles (*dvoryanstvo*), who were often educated in Europe and embraced European culture albeit sometimes quite superficially. They sometimes preferred to express themselves in German or, later, in French instead of Russian. Even the structure of their names was different. In earlier centuries it was customary to use a given name and a patronymic as a respectful form of address between adults. Now patronymics were reserved for the nobility. In relations between classes, full names almost disappeared, replaced by a derogatory nickname: Ivashka for Ivan, Onryushka for Andrey,

Glashka for Glafira, and so on. Catherine II forbade the use of such pejorative names for the higher classes and herself, but they were still widely used for serfs.

The nobles were the only ones to own land and peasants. Additionally, they did not pay any direct taxes and after 1762 were no longer obliged to serve the tsar. They could enjoy their lives in their rural estates or cities, or even moved abroad, living off the labour of their serfs, employing them as agricultural labourers, workers in factories or domestic servants.

In his book 'Russian History, a Very Short Introduction', Jeffrey Hosking, one of the best English historians of Russia, wrote that *'the nobles became the only estate to have guaranteed rights, and this fact meant that serfdom became even more arbitrary: serfs had no legal protection against abuse. Russia was now run by a ruling class with its own defined rights with a Europeanized culture, and complete power over the persons of its serfs. This internal cultural and social gulf defined Russian life for the next (nineteenth) century. The serfs for their part, were perfectly capable of discerning that, while they still had state obligations, their superiors had none.'*[6]

This social model was politically explosive. A small group of people, about 1% of the population, held about 95–97% of their fellow countrymen as slaves and shifted the entire tax burden onto peasants. The main tax was the poll tax, where every man (except the nobles) had to pay a fixed amount of money every year.

Peasants were the only ones required to serve in the military and were recruited for life until Emperor Paul limited service to 25 years. Landowners had to send a certain percentage of their male serfs to the army, causing family tragedies as wives and children were left without husbands and fathers for years. Special laws were adopted to deal with babies born to soldiers' wives while their husbands were away serving the tsar. Those children were considered illegitimate and were doomed to slavery. They belonged to the same landlord as their mothers even if their real fathers were free men or even nobles.

There was a cruel logic behind such organization of military service. The state was reluctant to arm or train the peasants, who were the only source of potential recruits as they made up the majority of the population. It was feared that if they came back to their villages after their service and were returned to serfdom, they might organize a revolt against their owners or the tsar. So, for conscripts there was no way back. The army was completely separated from the rest of society, and soldiers had to abandon their families for the rest of their lives. Officers, of course, were members of the nobility and were even allowed to stay with their wives and children in their estates when there was no military campaign. Soldiers, in their turn, spent their entire lives in barracks. The lyrics of a popular army marching song were a bitter testimony to the harsh reality of their existence: 'Loaded cannons are our wives, bombs and bullets are our kids…'. It's probably one of the most dreadful sides of Russian serfdom.

---

6   Geoffrey Hosking, *Russian History. A Very Short Introduction* (London: Oxford University Press, 2012), 48–49.

The state wanted its workforce to remain uneducated because education could lead to critical thinking, which was seen as a potential threat. Even knowledge of the Bible could raise questions about human rights, so the authorities kept the peasants illiterate and prevented them from reading the Holy Scriptures. In church, priests used to preach in Old Slavonic, a language that only specialists could fully understand. This was a deliberate attempt to have the population under control.

Most of Russians lived without freedom, civil rights, or legal protection. They were not allowed to own property and were at the mercy of their lords, who even had power over their families. They received no education and lacked strong moral values, unable to distinguish between right and wrong. Religious, if not Christian, values were not taught to them, despite their importance in shaping personal beliefs. Although some elements of traditional morality survived, they were weak. Government officials, including some emperors, were often aware of this dire situation, yet they chose to maintain the status quo.

At the turn of the 19th century, Alexander I ascended to the Russian throne. A highly educated monarch with modern ideas, he sought to establish law as the foundation of his state – 'Zakon' (law) was the word he ordered to be engraved on his coronation medal. And he worked tirelessly for this vision. He recognized the need to emancipate the peasants, but understood it wasn't possible without consent from the nobility, who depended on their labour. In March 1803, he proclaimed a special law that allowed landlords to free their peasants and grant them land. Giving them land was a mandatory condition of emancipation, unlike in some European countries where free peasants had nothing and became poor tenants of their former masters. The emperor's decree did not create an obligation, but merely suggested a possibility. He was surprised to learn that only a tiny proportion of the aristocracy, not more than one tenth of one percent, made use of it and freed some of their serfs. I myself was shocked when I learned that none of the noblemen who took part in the Decembrist revolt of 1825 had liberated their own peasants under this law. They put forward ideas of freedom, equality, fraternity, and human rights, praised the examples of republican France, the United States, and Great Britain, but failed to do as they preached. It is a poignant reminder that even highly educated Russians were often quite selfish in their actions.

Alexander I was committed to making the lives of the Russian people better, and he pursued various approaches to end the practice of serfdom. He recognized that soldiers had to live miserable lives and sought to improve their fate. To this end, he established military settlements where they could remain with their families and continue to work on the land. This effort was commendable, not only because families were no longer separated, but also because peasants received access to education. Schools for both children and adults, as well as medical hospitals, were established in these settlements. Furthermore, soldiers were allowed to possess weapons, which gave them a sense of autonomy and freedom.

Alexander I created a comprehensive education system, opening universities, gymnasiums, and real schools throughout the country. Nevertheless, access to those institutions was limited only to free members of society, and not to serfs, as Alexander was cautious not to jeopardize his relations with the nobility.

He annexed new territories, such as Finland in 1809, Bessarabia in 1812, and Poland in 1815, but agreed to establish local parliaments and representative self-government institutions there and supported their semi-autonomous status.

Despite Alexander I's efforts, he was not very successful in carrying out his reforms as the ruling nobility was largely against him. They had two different reasons for it. Firstly, young, educated aristocrats who had returned from Europe after the wars with Napoleon (the occupation of France by Russian troops ended in 1818), were dreaming of the liberation of Russia, but were less enthusiastic about setting their own serfs free. The older generation of the Russian nobility for their part wanted to keep things the way they were and to maintain serfdom without any changes.

Nicholas I, Alexander's brother and successor, was not as capable, well educated, or visionary. He made no significant effort to continue with the changes and during his reign from 1825 to 1855, Russia's development came to a halt. Whereas Alexander had commissioned the translation of the Bible into modern Russian and even published the New Testament and the Psalms, Nicholas I banned their sale and stopped further translation work. He also issued a decree forbidding peasants from attending gymnasiums or real schools, condemning them to a life without education or medical care.

The consequences of these policies were devastating. The first general population census was conducted in 1896–1897, almost 35 years after the abolition of serfdom, and provided honest and comprehensive data on life expectancy. The results were shocking, especially given that they covered all segments of the population, from peasants to town dwellers and nobles. On average, ethnic Russian men were expected to live no longer than 27.5 years while women had a life expectancy of 29.8 years. Other ethnic groups fared slightly better (see table below)[7].

Ethnic group	Average life expectancy, years	
	Men	Women
Bashkirs	37.2	37.3
Belarusians	35.5	36.8
Chuvash	31	31
Estonians	41.6	44.6
Jews	36.6	41.4
Latvians	43.1	46.9
Lithuanians	41.1	42.4

7   Бори́с Н. Миро́нов, *Социальная история России* (Санкт-Петербург: Дмитрий Буланин, 2000), Т.1, с.208.

Ethnic group	Average life expectancy, years	
	Men	Women
Moldavians	40.5	40.5
Tatars	34.6	35.1
Ukrainians	36.3	39.9

By comparison, in Sweden at that time, life expectancy was 52 for men and 55.5 for women. Even for the Neanderthals who lived around 150,000 years ago, it was 33 for men and 35 for women, longer than for Russians at the end of the 19th century. These figures speak for themselves and are a stark reminder of the brutal realities at that time.

In this text, I have been using the term 'empire' in its traditional sense, referring to a state that uses force of coercion to govern its territories. The word comes from the Latin root 'impero,' which means 'to rule' or 'to order'. So, an empire is a state built on the power of extortion, often against the will of its people.

Britain was also an empire, but life in England was very different from life in India, which was ruled from London. In England people were generally free. They elected their representatives to Parliament and had a government that looked after their interests. On the other hand, the Russian Empire is often referred to as a *prison of peoples*. While this is true, we must not forget that first and foremost, it was a prison for Russians themselves.

As an aside, I must say that we are currently witnessing a significant shift in the imperial attitude that has long prevailed in the West. Recently Rishi Sunak, a Hindu whose parents came from Punjab, was appointed Prime Minister of the United Kingdom. An event as important as the election of Barack Obama, an Afro-American, as President of the United States in November 2008.

To understand the Russian state is to understand its main founding principle, which was to use force to enable a small minority of the population to live off the labour of the vast majority. In essence, Russia was an empire designed to benefit the ruling nobility at the expense of the common people.

The Russian Empire didn't exploit just Poles, Chechens, Ukrainians, and Belarusians, but also Russians. Unlike them, some other ethnic groups, like Tatars, Bashkirs, Kalmyks, most peoples from Caucasus, and Jews were not even subjected to serfdom. Muslims were exempted from military service. This is one of the main reasons why Russians had a lower life expectancy than many other ethnicities. In contrast to Great Britain or Spain, which lived off distant colonies, the Russian Empire oppressed its own mainland population.

The need for reform was in the air, and Alexander I tried to bring about changes. However, his own success may have been the reason for his failure to achieve sustainable results. As a conqueror and victor over Napoleon, who liberated (or occupied, depending on one's perspective) Paris in 1814, he was the head of the Concert of Europe, saluted as 'king of kings' or 'Agamemnon of Europe' even by the British. It is possible that his triumph convinced his successor, Nicholas I, that Russia was already perfect and that nothing more needed to be done. After all, it was the strongest European country, or at least that was what he believed. Count Alexander Benckendorff, head of the gendarmerie and probably one of the emperor's closest confidants, is remembered to have said: 'Russia's past is remarkable, its present is nothing short of marvellous, and its future is beyond even the boldest imagination.' For the sake of appearances, Nicholas I established committees to consider the emancipation of serfs, but they did little, if anything.

On the ground, however, the reality was far from the ideal depicted in official reports. An astute Frenchman, Marquis de Custine, visited Russia in 1839 and wrote a two-volume book 'La Russie en 1839'. His observations are quite deep. He argued that a revolution in Russia was almost inevitable and would probably happen within 50 or 60 years. Although he got the timing wrong, his insights were right. The consequences of this 'frozen reign' were felt immediately.

Nicholas I launched an utterly immoral war against Turkey in 1853, for reasons that defy comprehension. A dispute arose over whether the Orthodox priests should continue to hold the keys to the main door of the Church of the Nativity in Bethlehem. The French demanded that the keys be given to the Catholics, and the Sultan of the Ottoman Empire agreed, entrusting them to the bishop of Palestine. This decision sparked a war, in which France, Great Britain, and the Kingdom of Sardinia sided with Turkey. The war proved disastrous for Russia: its army suffered a crushing defeat, and control of Sebastopol, the main Black Sea naval base, was lost. Nevertheless, it also opened the public's eyes to the dismal state of Russian society. This is reminiscent of the present day, when the world was surprised by the revelation that the Russian military is not as powerful or well equipped as President Putin used to claim.

To the astonishment of many, the Russian army of over a million soldiers proved to be weak and ill-equipped. Its weapons were outdated, with firearms from the Napoleonic Wars still in use, while French and British soldiers had access to modern rifles. Russian guns had a limited range of approximately 300 paces, whereas British rifles had a much greater range of 1200 paces and higher accuracy. Additionally, the Russian fleet was obsolete and lacked ironclad steamers, no match for the French and British warships. As a result, the war was lost, and Nicholas I died soon after the defeat at the age of 58. On a cold February day, when he went to greet new army platoons, he refused to put on a warm coat, caught a cold and died of pneumonia three weeks later. Many believed he had committed suicide, unable to bear the shame of his beloved army.

The Russian economy was also in tatters. At the beginning of the 19th century, during the reign of Alexander I, Russia smelted 5 kg of cast iron per capita. By 1850, this figure fell to 3.3 kg. Cast iron was then a symbol of national development, much like IT technologies are today. In addition, the per capita grain harvest gradually declined from 700 kg in 1820 to 580 kg in 1850. The Crimean War was a consequence of Russia's economic, social, legal, and political stagnation.

The army suffered from a shortage of gunpowder. Corruption was rife in the Ministry of Defence: soldiers often had to go into battle wearing boots with cardboard soles. This astonishing level of corruption was a direct result of absolutist rule, where society had no control over the bureaucracy. Slaves proved to be poor soldiers and inefficient workers. While other European countries had adopted free labour and recruited armies of free citizens, Russia's reliance on serfs caused it to fall further and further behind. This became clear to all of Europe during the Crimean War. A small joint British, French and Sardinian expeditionary force defeated the much larger Russian army and navy on Russian territory and in Russian territorial waters. This was not only a terrible shame but also a catalyst for reform.

The era of stagnation gave rise to Great Reforms as Alexander II, the son of Nicholas I, recognized the urgent need for action. He dreamed of profound, transformative change, and his reforms were remarkable. Although he may not have been an outstanding ruler himself, he was advised by a group of capable individuals. This group included his brother Konstantin, his aunt Elena (a German princess and the widow of his uncle Mikhail), and several members of the Russian nobility, such as the Milyutin brothers, Konstantin Kavelin, Senator Yakov Solovyov, Yakov Rostovtsev, Sergey Lanskoy, Yuri Samarin, Pyotr Valuyev, Alexander Koshelev, Sergei Zarudny, Dmitry Zamyatnin, Vladimir Butkov, and Count Mikhail Loris-Melikov. Although this circle was not large, it included some truly talented statesmen. Together, they set out to repair the fabric of the Russian society.

The idea of an Empire controlling the majority of the population for the benefit of a small minority had to be put to an end. All citizens of Russia, regardless of their ethnic origins, had to become free and enjoy equal rights, even if it was not immediately achievable. The first step had to be the emancipation of the serfs. Alexander II realized that taking land away from the nobility, who had been granted it in exchange for their service to the state, would be illegal, immoral, and inequitable. But slavery was inhumane, and the majority of serfs did not have the means to buy their own land. Although there were some wealthy peasants who owned small factories or commercial enterprises, they were rare exceptions. Following the example of the Habsburg monarchy in Hungary, where peasants had been liberated and given land in 1848, Alexander II issued a proclamation on February 19, 1861, granting personal freedom to all peasants and citizens of Russia.

All serfs, regardless of their owner, even those who belonged to the State or to the Tsar, were emancipated, and given their cattle and a small plot to live on for free. The land necessary for farming and pastures, however, had to be bought from their land-lords. As peasants had no money, the state let them borrow the necessary funds and gave them 49 years to repay the loan. The implementation of this scheme was not with-out challenges, as most of the nobles (around 60 or 70%) were against. They believed that if the serfs were to be freed at all, they should not be given any land. Only an ab-solutist monarch, in a system without a parliament, could successfully put such a plan into action. Interestingly, just for once the absolutist state model proved to be efficient.

Setting serfs free was not enough, it was also necessary to give common people the tools for self-government. Before the Great Reforms, self-government was limit-ed to the nobility and wasn't very broad. With the reforms, it was finally extended to the whole of society. Peasants and their former landlords worked together in elected assemblies (*zemstvo*), which existed on various levels. Self-government laws were passed in 1864 for districts and provinces, although only in approximately a-third of them, and in 1870 for cities, where they led to spectacular achievements. Many fine buildings were constructed and modern infrastructure, such as running water, sanitation systems, electric lighting, and public transportation, made its first ap-pearance at that time.

Legal reform was another crucial step and an absolute necessity. New independent courts were created. Judges were impartial and appointed for life, a significant limita-tion on absolute rule. Even the tsar had no power to dismiss a judge. A jury was intro-duced for ordinary citizens and used in almost all cases. Juries were elected by local self-government, giving peasants, ordinary townspeople, workers, and small mer-chants the opportunity to serve on them.

Another important reform was in the field of education. Everyone got right to be admitted to gymnasiums, real schools, or universities. As the population was still large-ly illiterate, the state asked recently created self-government institutions to open new schools. They provided basic education for thousands of people. The figure of a teacher embodied the spirit of the Great Reforms.

Medicine followed. For the first time in Russian history, a system of clinics, phar-macies, hospitals, maternity homes, and psychiatric asylums was established with the help of state subsidies. Modern medical care became accessible even in remote towns and villages. A doctor was as much a symbol of change in Russia as a teacher.

Russia is a huge country, so the transformations above were slow. In 1911, just a few years before the First World War, only 38% of Russian soldiers were literate. And they were not only peasants but came from all walks of life after a complete reorganization of the army, carried out by General Dmitry Milyutin. He abolished lifelong service and introduced a new form of conscription, in which those who had to serve were deter-mined by a random draw. It affected about 10% of the male population of relevant age, and the duration of service was limited to only a couple of years. It was a very impor-tant reform.

And at last, in 1876, the Bible was translated into Russian and made widely available. For the first time, many people were able to read the sacred text in their own language.

The Great Reforms brought rapid economic growth together with social and political improvements. Production of iron, coal, grain, and sugar increased rapidly, accelerating Russia's development. The reforms also led to significant population shifts, as many people left villages and moved into cities.

How to organize life in this very fast-moving society was another challenge. You may remember that stagnation was the main problem during the time of Nicholas I. In contrast at the end of the 19th and the beginning of the 20th century, Russian society was developing at a breakneck pace in all areas – from music and theatre to literature and philosophy, to exact and natural sciences. Names of Pyotr Tchaikovsky, Modest Mussorgsky, Leo Tolstoy, Fyodor Dostoevsky, Vladimir Solovyov, Anton Chekhov, Sofia Kovalevskaya and Dmitry Mendeleev are known throughout the world.

Although political systems tend to be conservative, Russia's profound social changes forced the government to adapt quickly. The reforms required skills for their implementation, but many people still lacked the knowledge and experience necessary to take part in administrative and political life.

Numerous newspapers and magazines provided a platform for the public expression of ideas. Sweeping reforms led to the emergence of new social currents, including socialists, who aspired to power, wanted to take the state into their own hands and to shape it according to their delusional ideas of social equality. Their radical proposals included taking all the land from the nobility and giving it to the peasants, confiscating the factories and passing control of them to the workers. Unfortunately, the people in general were still poorly educated and therefore had the habit of believing every printed word. This ended tragically on 1 March 1881, when Alexander II, known in Russian history as the Liberator, was assassinated by revolutionaries.

Just before his death, the tsar had been considering the establishment of a national parliament modelled on European examples. It would be a deliberative body, with representatives nominated by provincial assemblies and major cities. Although not as democratic as the British Parliament, it would still have been a significant step forward. It's symbolic that Alexander II signed the decree, creating the Council of State, at noon on March 1 and was killed just 2.5 hours later by members of the *Narodnaya Volya* (People's Will) terrorist movement.

His son and successor, Alexander III, reacted by trying to stop the reforms that he believed had led to the tragedy. Of course, it was not possible to abandon them on the spot and return the country to the times of Nicholas I, but their course was reversed, and the following 13 years are known as the era of counter-reform.

Nicholas II, the last tsar of Russia, followed in his father's footsteps, which eventually led to the revolution of 1905. People were fed up with the government's unpopular policies and the defeat in the war with Japan made things even worse. The revolution didn't overthrow the traditional Russian elite, but it did lead to the formation of a national parliament. Furthermore, the Manifesto, written by Prime Minister Sergey Witte and signed by Nicholas II on 17 October 1905, guaranteed political and civil rights and promised a constitution and an elected two-chamber parliament with broad powers.

On April 26, 1906, the first Russian Constitution, called the Fundamental Laws, was proclaimed. Russia became a constitutional monarchy and a parliamentary state, but the absolute power of the tsar still did not disappear. The struggle between the parliament and the tsar, and between society and the tsar, continued. Let's not forget that the Russian Empire was built on the exploitation of its own people, and this perception still shaped the views of the majority of the Russians, regardless of their level of education or their social class. They didn't feel connected to the state. 'God is high above and the Tsar is far away' was a popular saying. And this attitude was quite widespread: 'This country is not ours. The village we live in – yes, but the country belongs to the Tsar.'

Although the peasants had been given both freedom and land, they had not yet become citizens, as in Germany, France, or Great Britain. There was no developed sense of national identity. That's hardly surprising; where could it come from, in a country of former slaves, most of whom couldn't even read? The intellectuals, some 15–18% of the population, shared European values of nationalism, patriotism, liberalism, or socialism, while the majority, even after the October Manifesto, were focused on survival or blinded by the desire to get rich quickly. National interests were just empty words for them. The only thing they wanted was to get their hands on their former owners' lands and live as they pleased, enjoying all the modern benefits brought by self-government.

Pyotr Stolypin, Prime Minister and a brilliant politician, stated in 1910 that Russia needed two decades of peace to rebuild itself, so that ongoing transformations would bear fruit of new political forms. He himself worked hard to pass new laws to push the country forward. Vladimir Lenin, Stolypin's political adversary, wrote at the same time that if liberal reforms were to continue for another 15 years, revolutionaries would have no place in Russia. Smart people from opposing camps understood that a revolution was still possible because of rapid changes and lack of adequate social and administrative structures, but after fifteen or twenty years of successful reforms everything would change.

The common people would become true citizens and the absolutist Nicolas II would be succeeded by a new, modern-minded monarch who would agree to a truly constitutional system in which he would reign but not rule. The country would be ruled by educated people, through their accountable and freely elected representatives. All this would be the result of a natural evolution, because of an economically viable redistribution of property and better education. Such was the future dreamed of by Stolypin and feared by Lenin.

Stolypin was murdered in September 1911, and there were no prime ministers of his calibre after him. Russia did not get its twenty years of peace. Three years later, in 1914, Russian Tsar decided to go to war with Austria and Germany. The outcome of this war was terrible.

Lenin was biding his time.

Tragic Choices

In the second lecture, I gave a brief review of the key events in pre-revolutionary Russia. Our discussions focused on the emancipation of Russian society, which went far beyond the mere liberation of the serfs. Local self-government institutions were created, pre-censorship was abolished, and censorship, in general, became less strict. Independent courts appeared, including jury courts, where judges were appointed for life and protected by law from dismissal, which promoted a competitive judicial process and ensured the independence of the legal profession. Army underwent deep reforms, and universal conscription replaced the old system of forced military service. Education and health care became accessible for all. And last but certainly not least, the Bible was translated into modern standard Russian. The process started by Martin Luther in the 16th century reached Russia in the 1870s, and the Russian public could finally read the Hole Scripture in the language they could understand.

These events spurred an exceptionally rapid development of Russian society, fostering economic growth, social advancement, urban population expansion, and an increase in literacy rates. With regard to its economic progress, Russia was second only to the United States and on par with Sweden. In terms of total income, Russia ranked fourth, behind the United States, Great Britain, and Germany. By 1914, it accounted for 7.4% of world output. Its standard of living was still relatively low, with per capita income at $66 compared to $365 in the United States and $179 in Germany, but it was on a significant upward trajectory. The Russian economy made extraordinary progress in many sectors. For example, between 1894 and 1914, the production of iron and cast iron exploded thirteenfold, copper production quadrupled, coal production increased sixfold, and sugar and cotton production rose fourfold and sevenfold respectively. These figures testify to the remarkable expansion of the Russian economy.

I've already explained that Russia's difficulties during the Crimean war in the middle of the nineteenth century had been rooted in the stagnation of its economy and society, caused in their turn by serfdom and the absolutist practices of Nicholas I. The absence of self-government and the lack of effective oversight of the bureaucracy led to rampant corruption. The courts were plagued by bureaucratic red tape and outright bribery, while rigorous censorship extended not only to printed materials but also to university lectures and church sermons.

Suddenly Russia's problems were reversed. The economy was growing rapidly, but the development of political institutions and changes in public attitudes were not keeping pace. Until 1905, Russia remained an absolute monarchy, and even after the First Russian Revolution of 1905–1907, it was still a semi-absolutist state. Despite the establishment of a parliament, known as the State Duma and the State Council, the monarch retained control over the cabinet of ministers and the nation's financial system. It was an unusual symbiosis of a rapidly developing society with new-found political rights and a semi-absolutist imperial power.

The Russian Constitution of 23 April 1906 was often more liberal on civil rights than most other contemporary European fundamental laws. And there was a genuine effort to put these rights into practice. However, the Russian parliament had limited powers, as the government was appointed and controlled by the emperor and remained accountable to him. The rapid development of the nation, combined with the relative stagnation of the political institutions, posed a danger as the Russians began to realize that the country did not really belong to them, but to the tsar and the bureaucrats. The common people lacked the means to influence state policy.

In peacetime, Russia could have transitioned naturally and smoothly to a democratic system and become a parliamentary monarchy like Great Britain or Sweden somewhere by 1930 or 1940. But history did not give my country this chance. In 1910, Pyotr Stolypin predicted that all Russia needed to become a normal constitutional monarchy was 20 years of peace. Only four years later, Russia was at war. It was thrown into that war not by the decision of the tsar, but by the will of the people. Just as in 1877 before the war with Turkey, in 1913–1914 the majority of Russians, who were now more educated and socially active, succumbed to the same disease that afflicted the whole of Europe: nationalism. In Germany it was pan-Germanism, in the Turkic world it was pan-Turkism. In Russia it was pan-Slavism and pan-Orthodoxism if I may introduce this new term which seems appropriate here. Even Catholics in the Slavic provinces of the Austrian Empire, such as Bohemia, Moravia, Carniola (Slovenia), Croatia, not to mention Eastern Galicia and Bukovina with their substantial Orthodox population, felt a sense of unity with Russia because it was a Slavic and Orthodox state.

The reason for the war was a mistaken belief in the unity of all Slavs and Orthodox Christians based on language and religion. It was an illusion, because obviously Russians cannot understand either Serbian or Czech without assiduous study. Linguistic proximity, rather than a genuine sense of unity, led to an absurd sense of responsibility and an improbable claim to Russia's patronage and protection of the Slavic peoples of the Balkans and Central Europe. The common Orthodox Christian faith and the narrative of 'our Orthodox Slavic brothers' under attack, strangely enough became a rallying cry for war. Although, to be fair, Christianity, which has always proclaimed peace as the supreme good and the highest virtue, had often been used as a *casus belli* in Europe before. Let us recall, for example, the nightmare of the bloody Thirty Years' War (1618–1648), which claimed the lives of up to 40% of the population of Central Europe. At the beginning of the 20th century, however, any talks of a spiritual and political bond between the Slavs of Central Europe, the Balkans and Russia, who differed greatly in their social structures and ways of life, were highly implausible, to say the least.

From a non-populist perspective, it is not clear why perceived linguistic similarity should lead to political unity and the emergence of political ideologies like pan-Germanism, pan-Turkism, and pan-Slavism. Nevertheless, such ideas gained traction. And the catalyst that set things in motion was the assassination of Archduke Franz Ferdinand. We have evidence to believe that this murder was orchestrated by a Serbian terrorist organization known as 'Unification or Death', commonly referred to as the 'Black Hand'. The group's leadership was made up of Serbian police and army officers who had been involved in the assassination of Serbian King Aleksandar Obrenović in 1903. Subsequently, they gained influence under the new monarch, King Petar I (Petar Karadjordjević), who came to the throne through this violent coup. In 1914, Colonel Dragutin Dmitrijević, the head of Serbian military intelligence, took control of this secret organization.

Neither King Petar I nor Prime Minister Nikola Pašić actively pursued the idea of uniting all the southern Slavs from the Austro-Hungarian and Ottoman territories under Serbian leadership. It was the project of the secret service, whose aim was to overshadow Austria as a cultural and political centre of Slavic unification. In the years preceding the war, Austria had entertained the idea of transforming itself into a federation of several states. Interestingly, Archduke Franz Ferdinand and his Czech wife, Countess Sofia Chotek, were strong supporters of the idea. There were concerns that such a federation would be more appealing to the Slavs than Greater Serbia would be to the Croats, Bosnians, and Slovenes.

Dmitrijević's plans went even further than the creation of the Greater Serbia. He and his associates dreamed of eliminating King Petar and establishing their own Bonapartist dictatorship in the Balkans. The Archduke's fateful assassination was meticulously planned to satisfy these boundless personal ambitions. In the summer of 1917, all the organizers, including Colonel Dmitrijević were tried for high treason and executed by a Serbian court in Thessaloniki[8]. Nonetheless, the damage was done. The *Belle*

---

8   Андрей ЗУБОВ, "Кто хотел войны в 1914 г. и стал ли миром Версальский мир. Опыт сравнения с сегодняшним днем," *Новая газета* (September 2014). Available at https://novayagazeta.ru/articles/2014/09/13/61131-professor-andrey-zubov-prichiny-i-posledstviya-pervoy-mirovoy-voyny; John R. Lampe, *Yugoslavia as History: Twice There Was a Country* (New York: Cambridge University Press, 2000).

Époque came to its end. The world was thrust into a world war that brought immense suffering to tens of millions of people and led to the collapse of four empires – German, Austro-Hungarian, Ottoman, and Russian.

The tsar declared a state of mobilization, just like in Russia today, and the result of this mobilization was war with Germany and Austria, and later with Turkey. In the early days of August 1914, almost the whole of Europe was engaged in hostilities.

Initially the Russian public showed tremendous enthusiasm and support for the military actions, people still had good memories of Alexander II's victory over Turkey in 1878. The excitement was particularly palpable in large cities such as Petersburg, in the speeches of Duma deputies and on the pages of newspapers. Within two or three months, however, the thrill waned. The widespread belief that the coming war would be a walk in the park and that the Central Powers would soon be done with, faded with the first battles. The Russian army was defeated at Tannenberg in East Prussia and then suffered heavy losses during its retreat from Poland. By early 1915, the public mood had shifted from elation to deep disappointment. The once unshakeable belief in the invincibility of the Russian army was shattered. This change in attitude was caused not only by the tragedies of war and heavy casualties, but also and to a large extent by the absolutist practices of the state.

In a democratic country, the government is elected by the people and is expected to act in accordance with their interests. If it declares war, it's an expression of the collective will of the voters. In contrast, in an absolutist state like Russia, the foreign policy decisions were the prerogative of the emperor, as the Duma had no power to influence international affairs. Thus, any war was seen as the emperor's war. Military success would boost his popularity and win admiration for him. However, difficulties and casualties would lead to public disappointment and frustration. I think we are seeing a similar pattern in Russia today. The annexation of Crimea in 2014 was perceived as a triumph by the public and generated enthusiasm. But as the war drags on and casualties mount, disillusionment will set in. This may have happened in Russian in 1915 as well.

During the World War I, life in Russia, especially in the inland regions away from the front, was relatively good compared to Germany or Austria. There was an ample supply of basic food products and other commodities. However, after the defeats in 1915, a shift in the perception of the war occurred. People began to view it as a reckless scheme of an unsuccessful tsar rather than their own struggle. Russian soldiers, mainly peasants, were unwilling to spend years fighting instead of living peaceful lives in their villages. They didn't understand the purpose of the war and the reasons behind the Russian Tsar's conflict with the German Emperor and Austrian Kaiser.

General A. Brusilov, who commanded the south-west front, recalled: 'New soldiers arriving from the Russian interior had no understanding of the war that had come upon them out of the blue. Countless times I asked in the trenches why we were fighting, and the inevitable answer was that some archduke and his wife had been killed and because of this the Austrians wanted to take revenge on the Serbs. But hardly anyone knew who the Serbs really were; they had no idea who the Slavs were either, or why the Germans had decided to go to war over Serbia was completely beyond them. It turned out that people were being led to slaughter for reasons unknown to them, in other words, at the whim of the tsar.'

Although the military situation improved in 1916 compared to previous years, the social and political mood in the country went down. This was mainly due to the exhaustion from the war and the heavy losses suffered by the population.

Objectively, however, the situation on the fronts was unfavourable to the Central Powers. The expected quick victory did not materialize as France had not surrendered and the Russian armies, although in retreat, had continued to fight. By 1915, the German General Staff had come to the realization that it would be impossible to defeat the Entente powers solely on the battlefield, so they tried another tactic: subversion. They were not the only ones to think about it, as Russia, also resorted to similar moves by attempting to stir up unrest among the Slavic population within the Austro-Hungarian Empire. Also, Russia wasn't their only target, as the Germans also tried their hand in Britain and France. But the Russians turned to be far more receptive to such manipulations because of their belief that the war was not their own, yet exclusively the tsar's. We'll soon see how the Germans have been able to exert their influence, but let's first look at the prevailing political moods in Russia.

Liberal members of Russian society were also critical of the tsar, but for different reasons. They supported the war effort, but they were craving a democratic state, a constitutional monarchy. As a result, the tsarist regime had almost no popular support. Ordinary people were unwilling to fight for a cause that they found difficult to comprehend. Meanwhile, liberals, including some members of the ruling Romanov family, called for a parliamentary system and the abolition of semi-absolutist rule. They wanted a government that would be accountable to the State Duma, reflecting the will of the voters, rather than being solely under the control of the tsar.

In the early months of 1917, the military situation seemed under control. The country had managed to stabilize its borders, and the Russian industry was producing significant amounts of weapons and supplies. But discontent was brewing among the lower classes, who expected major changes in their lives and an end to the war. Meanwhile, the liberals wanted the war to continue, but under their control without the tsar's absolute rule.

There is another important reason, often overlooked, why people in Russia wanted the war to end as soon as possible. In the countryside, peasants still used to live in agrarian communities. Every twelve years, the land in the village would be redistributed among the families to take account of births, deaths, and changing needs. One such redistribution took place in 1905, the year of the First Russian Revolution, and the next one was planned for 1917.

Most of the soldiers were peasants. They understood that if they remained in the army, land would be reallocated in their absence, potentially to the advantage of those who stayed in the villages, as their wives alone would be unable to protect their interests. As a result, soldiers were anxious to return to their homes to take part in the redistribution of land. It was a matter of a very serious concern for them.

When assessing the motivation of an army, an important factor to consider is the ratio of casualties to captured prisoners of war. If it is low, i.e. more POWs are captured for every soldier killed or wounded, it may be a sign of a potential problem, an indication of a lack of resolve or willingness to fight.

Country	Killed (1)	Wounded (2)	POW (3)	Ratio (1 + 2) / 3
Russia (before March 1918)	1,650,000	3,850,000	2,400,000	2.3
Germany	1,808,545	4,247,143	617,992	9.8
Austria-Hungary	1,200,000	3,620,000	2,200,000	2.2
France	1,385,000	3,044,000	446,000	9.9
Great Britain	947,000	2,122,000	192,000	16.0

As you can see the ratio of casualties to POWs in different countries during the World War I varied considerably. In the British army, it was 16, meaning that for every 16 soldiers wounded or killed, one was taken prisoner. In France it was 9.9, in Germany 9.8, in the Austro-Hungarian Empire 2.2 and in Russia 2.3. The figures for Austria and Russia are similar, but the reasons behind them are different.

In the Austro-Hungarian Empire, many soldiers of Slavic origin did not want to fight the Russians. Some even crossed the frontline to join the Russian army. It was not the case in Russia. There wasn't any significant support for enemy countries. Lots of soldiers simply didn't want to continue a war they did not consider their own.

In France, Great Britain, and Germany, where the proportion of casualties to POW was higher, the war was seen as a national cause and not just the fight of their leaders. For Russians, however, it was the tsar's war, and many felt no personal connection to it.

As always there were political forces trying to capitalize on public sentiment. In Russia, during 1917, the struggle for political influence was mainly between two groups, both opposed to the Tsarist regime.

The first group represented the educated classes and consisted of liberal and left-liberal parties such as the Octobrists (Union of October 17) and the Constitutional Democratic (or People's Freedom) Party, also known as the Kadets, both represented in Duma.

The second group consisted of socialists who wanted not only to dismantle the existing regime but to completely transform the Russian society. They called for the convening of a Constituent Assembly, with the aim of rebuilding the state from the ground up. The socialist movement was influential and widespread throughout the whole Europe at that time.

The majority of socialists in Russia, as in Germany or Austria wanted to establish a truly democratic political system that would allow the participation of all members of society, including the poor, the uneducated and the women. Their goal was to win democratic elections and use the democratic mandate to build a socialist state in which the people would collectively control property through democratic processes. In Russia, parties such as the Mensheviks and Popular Socialists embraced this vision.

There were two other forces pulling in opposite direction. The Socialist Revolutionary Party (SR) wanted to come to power by democratic means and then seize all the arable land from the wealthy landowners and redistribute it to the peasants. Their intention was not to give the peasants private property, but to nationalize all agricultural land and to rent it out to the peasants for free. In a different vein, the Bolsheviks, led by Lenin, believed that it was necessary to seize power by force, to establish a dictatorship in order to bring about the necessary social changes. 'Political power grows out of the barrel of a gun,' as Mao Zedong famously summed such approach later.

The idea of a dictatorship did not enjoy widespread support. Having had enough of absolutism, the people were not interested in replacing one absolute ruler with another, whether it was Lenin or anyone else. Recognition and respect for their rights were what they sought. Few people understood what democracy was, but they all wanted equality and fairness, as pre-revolutionary Russia was still often marked by injustice. This is the reason why the Bolsheviks continued to call themselves 'social democrats', in an attempt to hide their anti-democratic authoritarian ideology.

The challenges of war intensified the activity of all political factions in Russia. Ordinary people, especially soldiers, more often aligned themselves with the socialists rather than with the liberals. We can understand why. As a predominantly agrarian nation, Russia's greatest asset was its arable land. Following the emancipation of the serfs, peasants were given individual ownership of their land. Unlike many European countries, where large tracts of land were owned by large landlords, Russia had a much bigger number of small private landowners. The Russian peasantry had a singular ambition: to regain control of all the land that still remained in the hands of the ruling family, landlords and merchants.

The proportion of such land was relatively small, only about eight or nine per cent. But most people didn't really care about it. As a result, political forces that promised land redistribution enjoyed widespread support, especially among the poorly educated or completely illiterate. Only two political groups advocated such radical measures: the Socialist Revolutionaries and the Bolsheviks. Of course, a shake-up of property rights of this scale carried the potential for disastrous consequences.

Ownership of factories was another contentious issue. The idea that workers themselves should own and manage the factories and plants was gaining ground.

Peace was also a pressing concern. There was a strong support for putting an immediate end to the war, a desire widely shared by population at large, soldiers, and military personnel. People wanted to save their lives and return to their villages in time for land reallocation.

All such claims were simply impossible, politically educated individuals understood this quite well. It was impossible to stop the war immediately, as it required an international conference, a challenge to organize when countries were still fighting, and each side was hoping to win. It was impossible to give all the land to the peasants without ruining the economy, and the same can be said of changing the ownership of factories. But the socialist parties made bold statements promising all of the above and instantly gained great popular support. Had Russia enjoyed a long tradition of democracy and liberalism with greater respect for people's rights, the extremely left Socialist propaganda wouldn't have been so successful. But Russia was not a democratic country and most of its citizens were still politically ignorant.

Mass demonstrations against the war began in Petersburg in the second half of February 1917. They soon escalated into mob violence against the police, and brutal reprisals followed. By the end of the month, the authorities had lost control of the situation in the capital. Nevertheless, the army at the front continued to obey orders from the Supreme Commander's Headquarters (Stavka), where Nicholas II had arrived. Given the situation, however, the emperor decided to renounce the throne both for himself and for his son Alexei, in flagrant violation of existing legislation[9].

The liberal factions that took charge after the tsar's abdication on 2 March 1917 were unable to maintain control of the country for long. They were gradually forced to cede power to the socialists, who enjoyed the overwhelming support of the majority. With soldiers refusing to continue fighting, especially after the abdication, Russia was forced to gradually withdraw from the war. This period, from March to November 1917, was marked by dramatic changes. Liberal democratic ideals lost their appeal, while socialist ideas gained considerable ground.

People could not grasp the absurdity of socialist promises because they could not understand that they were impossible to fulfil. In the early 20th century, many countries around the world were still struggling to understand that Marxist socialism, however appealing it might be to many, was merely an abstract concept, a set of meaningless phrases and slogans. Some more conscientious socialists who argued for cautious preparations for peace talks, rather than an immediate end to the war, were quickly marginalized from the political landscape and replaced by radicals.

The people placed their trust in the Constitutional Assembly, dominated by radical socialists, and expected it to build a new world by giving land to the peasants, granting

---

9   Андрей Зубов (ed.), *История России. XX век* (Москва, 2016). Т 1, с. 476–496.

factories to the workers, and securing a just peace without annexations or indemnities. From March to November, the Bolsheviks made three attempts to seize power. They tried first in April, and then at the beginning of July, but were unsuccessful. Both attempts were generously financed with large amounts of German money, which was used to win the support of soldiers and the general population.

Back then, before the internet, computers and radio, newspapers were the main source of information. The Bolsheviks' leading newspaper, Pravda (Truth), and its various versions, Soldatskaya Pravda (Soldiers' Truth) and Okopnaya Pravda (Trench Truth), experienced a significant surge in popularity. In April their daily circulation reached 25,000 copies, rising to 100,000 in May and finally to 350,000 in early July. The spread of Bolshevik propaganda through these newspapers gained momentum in the months between February and November. Their influence extended far and wide, reaching even the illiterate who relied on their more educated friends to read the texts to them. The simple language and persuasive messages of Bolshevik newspapers and leaflets appealed to many.

The publication of hundreds of thousands of newspapers required substantial financial support, which did not come from within. Instead, the funds came from Germany and Austria. They were used for propaganda, agitation, and the salaries of the Red Guards[10]. It was only after the World War II, when the archives of the German Ministry of Foreign Affairs were captured and subsequently made public by the Americans, that the mechanism of money transfers to the Bolsheviks became clear. Evidence sufficient to try and hang both Lenin and Trotsky for high treason under Article 108 of the Criminal Code of the Russian Empire came too late.

In 1958 Professor Zbyněk Zeman published a compilation of selected documents. The German Under Secretary of State, concerned about the arrests of the Bolsheviks, wrote to the German Minister in Copenhagen: 'The suspicion that Lenin is a German agent has been energetically countered in Switzerland and Sweden at our instigation. Thus the impact of the reports on this subject supposedly made by German officers has also been destroyed.' On September 3, after the German capture of Riga, the German State Secretary reported to the General Headquarters: 'The military operations on the Eastern front, which were prepared on a large scale and have been carried out with great success, were seconded by intensive undermining activities inside Russia on the part of the Foreign Ministry. [...] Our work together has shown tangible results. The Bolshevik movement could never have attained the scale or the influence which it has today without our continual support.'[11]

---

10   Виктор И. Кузнецов (ed.), *Тайна Октябрьского переворота: Ленин и немецко-большевистский заговор. Документы, статьи, воспоминания* (Санкт-Петербург: Алетейя, 2001); Winfried Baumgart, *Deutsche Ostpolitik 1918. Von Brest-Litowsk bis Zum Ende des Ersten Weltkrieges* (Munich: R. Oldenbourg Verlag. 1966), p.357.

11   Zbyněk A. B. Zeman (ed.), *Germany and the Revolution in Russia 1915–1918. Documents from the Archives of the German Foreign Ministry* (London: Oxford University Press, 1958).

The Red Guards were paid in counterfeit Russian roubles printed in Germany. The soldiers were quite happy to take them. I don't mean that the revolution was made with German money, that would be a mistake. Most Russians were looking forward to miraculous social transformations and a magical end to the war. This was not possible, but the radical socialists promised the impossible. Russia is a huge country and spreading their message required intense and costly propaganda work, so Lenin quite shamelessly took money from Russia's enemies, the Central Powers, who were happy to oblige.

Almost everyone believed that the Socialists, and especially the Bolsheviks, would change people's lives completely for the better. The war would end, peasants would be given land, there would be plenty of food and a peaceful future for all. On November 7, the Bolsheviks seized control in Petersburg in a carefully orchestrated coup d'état. The revolution spread quickly across Russia and within just a week the entire country was in flames.

Before these events, soon after the abdication of the Emperor, when the Provisional Government was in power, preparations began for elections to the Constituent Assembly. When the Bolsheviks finally seized power in November, they were unable to cancel or manipulate the upcoming elections (as Putin is free to do in Russia today). The vote was held in November 1917, just three weeks after the Bolsheviks took control.

The results were both revealing and impressive. Despite the country being in the midst of a revolution and a war, turnout was remarkably high, 62%. The Bolsheviks won 23.7% of the vote, a significant proportion but far from an overwhelming victory. The social revolutionaries, including their regional factions of Ukrainians, Muslims, and Siberian Kazakhs, together secured 59% of the total vote, forming a majority.

The Mensheviks suffered a major setback, receiving only 2.1% of the people's votes. The socialists advocating for democratic changes failed to gain significant support despite their active campaigning. The Constitutional Democrats, the only liberal party, only managed to win 4.8%. In larger cities such as Moscow and Saint Petersburg, their support was higher, reaching 30% and in some cities almost 60%. In the rural areas, however, no one voted for them, because they supported land redistribution by legal means with compensation for landowners. The peasants, seeking immediate change, failed to understand the need to respect legal procedures. They wanted everything and wanted it right away.

Right-wing parties won 3%. The monarchists didn't participate, but some Christian parties did. The Bolsheviks and other social revolutionaries were theomachists, openly hostile to any religious views and rejecting the idea of God altogether. Atheism was considered one of the principles of democracy. Lenin himself used the word 'God' in a derogatory way, referring to it by the diminutive 'bozhenka'. Most Bolsheviks and Socialist revolutionaries followed suit and took a similar position.

There were Muslim parties as well, representing the Tatars and the peoples of Central Asia, although they were more ethnic than religious in their views. Russia was predominantly a Christian state. Interestingly, in Ukraine, European Russia, and Siberia, there were different Christian Orthodox parties, representing both the Old Believers and the New Believers, but they collectively received only 1.7%. We can therefore conclude that less than 2% of the Russian population, in a context where atheism was prevalent, voted for religious parties.

This observation is quite significant. We are seeing a major decline in religious belief and practice. This is particularly evident when we look at the figures for participation in the Eucharist. Before the February Revolution of 1917, it was compulsory for Russian soldiers, mostly Orthodox Christians, to take part in the Eucharist at least once a year. Soldiers had to go to church and receive communion. As I mentioned earlier, more than two and a half million Russian prisoners of war found themselves in camps in Austria and Germany. The Hague Convention allowed them to practise their own faith. Priests visited them, conducted services, and administered the Eucharist. Surprisingly, only about 10% of the soldiers in these camps attended services, with the remaining 90% opting out. After the revolution only 1% of them continued to go to church and receive communion. This suggests that the percentage of the Russian population actively practising Orthodox Christianity at the time was around 1%. This figure is consistent with the proportion of voters who supported Christian parties in elections. It's important to note that the situation regarding religious beliefs and practices would undergo further changes in the communist future. We will discuss it in the next lecture.

After analysing the election results, Oliver H. Radkey wrote, 'These figures tell us a great deal. They reveal in stark outline certain of the fundamental weaknesses of Old Russia: the numerical insignificance of the middle class, the loss of vitality of once powerful institutions like the monarchy and the church, and the absence of a strong national consciousness such as had come to the rescue of Western conservatism when the old mainstays of monarchism and clericalism began to give way.'[12]

The Constituent Assembly was elected and convened for its first and last session on 5 January 1918. It met for twelve hours and was eventually dissolved by the Bolsheviks, who had full control of the state. The dissolution of the Constituent Assembly was a significant turning point, signalling the end of democracy in Russia and the establishment of a Bolshevik dictatorship.

Let us now try to uncover the motives behind the seizure of power by Lenin and the Bolsheviks, the dissolution of the democratically elected Constituent Assembly and their subsequent rule as dictators. Renowned Russian-born Yale historian George Vernadsky explored this very question in his book, 'Lenin: The Red Dictator.'[13] Was it to help the ignorant and uninformed masses? To lead the people towards a more prosperous life? Or were they solely driven by a thirst for power, using it to advance their

---

12   Oliver H. Radkey, *Russia goes to the polls: the election to the all-Russian Constituent Assembly, 1917* (Ithaca: Cornell University Press, 1989), p. 20.

13   George Vernadsky, *Lenin: Red Dictator* (New Haven: Yale university Press, 1931).

own agenda forgetting about the ordinary people who had supported them? Vernadsky, along with many other historians specializing in twentieth-century Russia, argued that the Bolshevik leaders were fanatically committed to communist ideology. They wanted to build a Marxist utopia on Earth, whatever it took, even if that meant committing atrocities. But was this really so?

The answer would be of immense importance, as it could help us understand all the subsequent events in Russian history, from 1917 to the present day. For Russia is still grappling with this legacy, even though its ideological Communist foundations are a thing of the past. We will try to find an answer in our next three lectures. But before that let's look at the general context.

The people wanted the war to be brought to an end. Did Lenin stop it? No. Worse, in his theoretical writings he argued that it was necessary to turn the imperialist war into a civil one, and that's exactly what happened. Russia was plunged into a devastating civil strife for five years, from 1917 to 1922. Approximately twelve million lives were lost due to combat, as well as the horrors of the Red Terror, famine, and epidemics. This casualty counts far surpassed the losses suffered during the World War I, in which some three and a half million Russians were wounded or killed. Tragically, internal violence proved even more devastating for the population than the 'imperialist' war.

The people wanted land. Did the peasants get it? At first sight, yes; but upon careful examination, no. After 1863, the peasants did indeed get land as their private property, after all it was one of the main ideas of the Great Reforms. But immediately after taking power on 8 November 1917, Lenin, with the support of the Socialist Revolutionaries, declared the abolition of all private land ownership in Russia and the *socialization* (nationalization) of all land.

What did *socialization* actually mean? In essence, it was the transfer of all property rights to those in power. Private property ceased to exist on the day of the Bolshevik coup. The peasants were given some land that had previously belonged to landlords and merchants, but only as temporary holdings, they didn't own it as before. Unfortunately, most peasants failed to see the difference. Worse still, it is fair to say that the country was thrown in its development back to the early 18th century: in the time of Peter the Great, all property was owned by the tsar. In 1762, Peter III granted land ownership to the nobility, while in 1803 Alexander I extended it to all free people. Finally, in 1861, Alexander II emancipated all the serfs and granted them land, either in individual or collective ownership. On 8 November 1917, however, private land ownership was abruptly abolished, and the only beneficiaries were the leaders of the Bolshevik Party.

The same fate befell the workers. In the immediate aftermath of the revolution, the factories were indeed handed over to them, but only for a short period of two or three months. The state soon regained control, and when workers in St Petersburg and Moscow began to assert their rights, demanding fair wages and other benefits, they were met with violent repression. A notable example is the Kronstadt rebellion in March 1921, where workers lost all the rights they had enjoyed before the revolution. Strikes were banned, independent workers' organizations were suppressed and there was no room for any form of democracy. Even socialist parties that had participated in the work of the *Soviets* (administrative assemblies or councils) were only allowed to operate until June 1918. From then on, all remaining non-Bolshevik groups were outlawed, effectively silencing any opposition. Non-socialist groups had already been dismantled by the end of 1917.

There was no bread to feed the hungry. The Bolsheviks banned all trade. It became impossible to buy goods in towns and cities. Then they tried to seize all the resources produced by the peasants. In practice, this meant that forced labour, which had been so widespread before the Great Reforms, was reintroduced in the spring of 1918. Peasant property, including staple foods for their own consumption, was confiscated. Large-scale hunger ensued. In a country torn apart by a civil war, many people died not from the fighting, but from starvation. Famine was the Bolsheviks' grim gift to the people.

Another important aspect to consider is personal safety and the value of human life. Under the Tsarist regime in the late 19th and early 20th centuries, around three thousand people were sentenced to death. At the beginning of their rule in September 1918, the Bolsheviks officially declared a policy of Red Terror. The power to execute people without any legal process was vested in the hands of the *Cheka*, a Special Commission tasked with enforcing revolutionary principles. No fewer than two million people were killed before the end of the Red Terror in 1921.

It is clear that Lenin acted in direct contradiction to the promises he had made during the revolution. His actions were driven not by a desire to improve people's lives, but by a wish to preserve his own power.

Vasily Maklakov, one of the leaders of the People's Freedom Party, and ambassador of the Provisional Government and the White Movement in France, wrote later in his European exile: 'After six months of system demolition, the Bolsheviks, in a very down-to-earth manner, ultimately recreated it along the lines of the old autocratic model, not so different from the traditional monarchy. It was possible because of our backwardness and servility. [...] Bolshevism has led Russia astray from its true path and permanently destroyed what was naturally valuable and sane there.'[14]

The Bolsheviks appropriated magnificent palaces, luxurious cars and whatever else they wanted for their personal use. Trotsky travelled in the tsar's special train, while Lenin stayed in the grand country palace of the Moscow governor-general. The Bolshevik leaders put their own lifestyles ahead of the welfare of the people in whose name they claimed to have made the revolution.

---

14   Василий А. Маклаков, *Власть и общество на закате старой России. Воспоминания современника* (Москва: НЛО, 2023), с. 35–36.

Mikhail Artsybashev, a well-known writer who had lived under Bolshevik rule until 1923, wrote in exile:

'Sincere fanaticism, no matter how insane, instils a certain respect. Even the gravest of crime, if perpetrated in the name of a great idea, driven by a genuine belief in the righteousness of one's cause, may be to some extent justified. [...] But I accuse the Bolsheviks of not being sincere fanatics, of being nothing more than mercenaries of the Revolution, a band of political opportunists consumed by personal greed and lust for power. For fanaticism is only about one's own idea. It makes the prophet march ahead of those he sends to Calvary. The Bolsheviks instead, crucified the Russian people, inflicting untold suffering, all in order to divide the spoils among themselves'. [...]
At the time when the people were starving, freezing and dying, when they were on the limits of grief and despair, the Bolshevik gang indulged in some bacchanalian funeral feast. [...] The communist comrades supplied themselves with everything, from white bread to caviar and wine, while doing everything possible to drive the people to hunger and desperation, making them risk their lives for each new piece of bread. They were quite reluctant to share the fate of those in whose name they ruled. [...] Selfless fighters for the common good as they were, they shamelessly enjoyed lavish bounties from huge food reserves built up at the expense of the starving. The Bolshevik clique revelled in a life of opulence, pleasure and drunkenness. But the Kremlin overlords even managed to outdo them in both comfort and debauchery. They had at their disposal the palaces of the Moscow tsars, the finest hotels, cars, precious furs, diamonds, vast quantities of gold, wine and women. Their corruption, fraud, wealth, gambling, drunkenness and debauchery were known throughout Russia, but the people remained silent, threatened with a 'cheka' revolver'.[15]

These claims are backed up by documents from the Kremlin archives, which only became accessible in the 1990s. For example, in November 1920, when much of Russia was suffering from hunger and cold, Lenin's family of three with servants received 24.5 kg of meat, 60 eggs, 7.2 kg of cheese, 1.5 kg of butter, 2 kg of black caviar, 4 kg of fresh cucumbers, over 30 kg of flour and grain, 5 kg of sugar, 1.2 kg of pastille candies, 1 kg of lard, and 100 cigarettes[16]. The other Bolshevik leaders were not far behind. For their summer holidays in 1924, Stalin and Dzerzhinsky got 5,000 gold roubles (average worker's monthly wage was 20–30 gold roubles, even the most skilled workers rarely earned as much as 50), Zinoviev and Trotsky 12,500 roubles. Stalin complained to Molotov about this 'injustice'[17]. These sums were kept hidden from public knowledge.

---

15   Михаил П. Арцыбашев, *Показания по делу Конради. Красный террор в Москве* (Москва: Айрис Пресс, 2010), с. 462–463.

16   Russian State Archive of Socio-Political History, fund Ф17, inventory Оп.84, Document Д.111, p. 8 (reverse)–9

17   Russian State Archive of Socio-Political History, fund Ф558, inventory Оп.1, Document Д.766, pp. 18–19

It would be inaccurate, however, to portray the Bolsheviks as primitive hedonists who deceived and killed countless people so that they could continue to live in opulence. Living in luxury was an important prerequisite (and they all enjoyed it to the full), but it was not their only motivation I'm afraid.

We'll try to explore the motives that moved Lenin and the Bolsheviks in more detail and will try to make them clear in our next lecture.

Nature of Bolshevik Power

What is Communist Russia? Any attempt to answer this question would inevitably lead us into a highly dramatic and serious discussion. For our ability to make an accurate assessment of the present-day Russia depends on our grasp of the nature of a communist state and of its ideology. Richard Pipes, a renowned historian, argues that the whole period of the Russian Revolution spanned from the early 20th century to 1924. His monumental three-volume work, *The Russian Revolution*, is the most comprehensive study of the subject written in any language[18]. Although we refer to it as 'Russian', it is important to recognize these events transcended national boundaries.

The coup of October 1917 is shrouded in myth. Some experts still believe that it was a momentous and glorious event in the development of Russia, and perhaps the world. The Russian Revolution is sometimes seen as a transition towards a new stage and the culmination of the historical process in the spirit of Hegel's philosophy of history[19].

In a sense, we can call it a great event, although we should understand its greatness in a different way. It served as a wake-up call to all European politicians, warning them of the urgent need for a more socially just state to prevent similar revolutions in their countries. It paved the way for a new political consciousness throughout Europe. Voting rights were extended in democratic nations, giving all citizens, especially those who had been marginalized and economically disadvantaged, the right to be heard. The popularity of labour parties increased.

Pyotr Chaadaev, a prominent 19th-century Russian philosopher, postulated in one of his articles that perhaps Russia exists only to teach the world an important lesson. A man of remarkable wisdom, he is widely regarded as one of Russia's greatest thinkers. He was officially declared insane and put under house arrest for his bold ideas.

---

18   Richard Pipes, *The Russian Revolution* (New York: Alfred A. Knopf, 1990); *Russia Under the Bolshevik Regime: 1919–1924* (New York: Alfred A. Knopf, 1993).

19   See different views in Martin Malia, *Comprendre la révolution russe* (Paris: Éditions du Seuil, 1980).

But he was right. Russia did indeed teach the world a lesson through the revolution. It was not about a bright and promising future. It was a warning against certain actions and policies. The Russian example served as a compelling reminder to steer clear of an over-fragmented society torn apart by enormous social divisions.

This was the first insight of the Russian Revolution: if the rulers fail to support the lower strata of society, there is a potential for some people to exploit the grievances of the wider population and to seize power, as happened in Russia.

There were other more positive consequences for the rest of the world. Many educated people who understood the nature of the communist regime early enough chose to flee the country. Their skills and talents enriched foreign countries. For Russia itself though, the revolution brought nothing but darkness and misery. And its negative effects have not yet been fully understood by the Russian people.

In this lecture we will try to uncover the true sense and meaning of the Bolshevik movement and the Communist regime in Russia. Let us always remember the words of Jesus Christ from the Holy Gospel: 'Ye shall know them by their fruits.' It means, that we gain insight into people's real beliefs and intentions by examining their actions. The Bolsheviks came to power in November 1917. From the beginning they made it clear that their ambitions extended far beyond Russia. Lenin, Trotsky and their comrades did not even think about improving the lives of the people. Instead, they wanted to use the country as a base for a world revolution leading to a world communist state.

They didn't need a world dominance to bring prosperity and freedom to the poor. Their aim was simple: to consolidate power over as much territory and as many people as possible. Sure, the Bolsheviks talked a lot about the wonders the future would bring, but they did nothing to improve people's lives. Instead, they put a lot of effort into creating a military machine to conquer other nations. The right to a happy, prosperous life, as I tried to show in my previous lecture, was reserved for themselves and their families. So, let's not believe their empty rhetoric, but look at what the Bolsheviks really did.

As an aside, it is worth noting that Nazism, another totalitarian movement of the first half of the 20th century, was far more transparent in its ideas than Bolshevism. Hitler was more direct and outspoken than Lenin in articulating his principles. He openly proclaimed the superiority of the German race, the 'real Arians', and claimed that they should rule the world. According to Hitler, other nations were inferior and destined to be subjugated by the Germans. He specifically targeted the Jews as enemies to be exterminated. The Nazis rejected democracy altogether, claiming that the Führer, was above all laws[20]. The Bolsheviks instead tried to conceal their intentions and cloak them in liberal rhetoric.

---

20   See Norbert Frei, Der *Führerstaat. Nationalsozialistische Herrschaft 1933–1945* (Munich: dtv, 1987). Translated into English as *National Socialist Rule in Germany: The Führer State 1933–1945*. Translated by Simon B. Steyne. (Oxford, Cambridge: Blackwell Publishers, 1993).

From Lenin to the end of their rule, the Bolsheviks loved to talk about democracy and the future prosperity of all nations and peoples. They also declared that a 'dictatorship of the proletariat' was essential to the success of the revolution. The precise definition of the 'proletariat' remains elusive. In ancient Rome it used to mean the lowest social class, but surely Lenin had a different interpretation in mind. He never really meant 'the rule of the disadvantaged'. His 'dictatorship of the proletariat' was in practice the dictatorship of the party leaders. Democracy and empowering of the poor were mere deceptions. Their ideology is full of similar lies, of words without real meaning. This was true in 1917, and it is true today.

Some of the actions of the Bolsheviks are now often seen as mistakes. In reality, they were not simple missteps, but deliberate and calculated strategies to build a totalitarian state.

They started by confiscating all private property. This was no accident. Those who own property and enjoy the freedom to use it for their own benefit are independent and self-reliant. They don't need mercy from the state, but rather the state itself exists only thanks to their taxes. It is impossible for an authoritarian government to control such potentially free individuals with independent income; they are unlikely to willingly join the ranks of the soldiers of a 'world revolution'. Free people may follow the communists, or they may as well reject their ideas. But for the Bolsheviks it was necessary to ensure everyone's obedience. To do this they needed absolute power over people's lives. The state had to become the sole source of people's livelihood.

So, the communist coup began with the confiscation of all private property. In the early years of the Bolshevik dictatorship, from 1918 to 1920, numerous decrees were issued declaring that all forms of property, including money, land, rural estates and urban residences, were to be owned by the state.

In anticipation of the socialization of property, on 15 December 1917, the Supreme Soviet of National Economy was created. On December 27, all banks were nationalized. On December 30, 1917, the Bolsheviks issued a decree to nationalize bank deposits, as well as jewellery and securities kept in bank vaults. Safes were broken into, valuables were seized for the needs of the revolution, cash withdrawals were suspended. The possessions that people had accumulated over generations were declared 'national property', that is, the property of the leadership of the Bolshevik Party. Money in bank accounts disappeared, dividends on shares were confiscated and transactions in securities stopped. Virtually everyone in Russia, from peasants to factory workers to state officials, used to keep their money in their bank accounts, so the decree of December 17 robbed practically everyone. The movable and immovable property seized by the Bolsheviks has never been returned to the rightful owners or their descendants.

On 13 January 1918, the Supreme Soviet declared that the new government would not honour state loans and refused to pay the debts of previous Russian administrations, thus denying all financial responsibility. At the same time, Lenin submitted a proposal to the Presidium of the Supreme Soviet for the widespread nationalization of production facilities. In a cynical tone he declared, 'Yes, we are robbing the robbers,' adding that this was the essence of the Bolshevism.

What followed is known as the 'Red Guard attack on capital'. Many factories closed and unemployment soared. But Lenin was undeterred. In the winter and spring of 1918, he issued a series of decrees targeting specific enterprises. Soon the river and sea merchant fleet and the private railways were nationalized. Property transactions were banned in December 1917, and in the following months the buying and selling of businesses was prohibited and inheritance rights abolished. Finally, on 28 June 1918, the nationalization of large industries was announced.

In August 1918, all real estate was declared state property. Former owners became tenants of the state. The authorities had the power to arbitrarily cancel leases and seize all or part of property at their discretion. In essence, communist Russia was controlled by a small group of revolutionary leaders who could effectively manage all confiscated assets and to distribute them to whomever they wished.

Many people were in need of means of subsistence (peasants needed land and city dwellers lacked places to live), and they appealed to the authorities for help. It's important to remember, however, that everything they received from the state, from land to housing, was not given in permanent ownership, but rather as temporary possessions. In the cities, the homeless took over houses, apartments, furniture and clothes from their previous owners with the permission of the new government. Such permissions were easily granted, as were warrants to search and requisition any 'surplus' property. Those who confiscated the property were well aware that they were committing a crime under the Russian law (and universal legal principles in general), and that they would be held accountable in the event of a change of power. That's why they started to align themselves with the communist regime. Property confiscation and redistribution became the first step in winning popular support.

The next step was to ban all trade. In 1918, all commercial activity came to a halt. Nobody could buy or sell anything; goods were distributed by the state instead. It's no surprise that this led to widespread hunger and starvation. To enforce this, special groups called food requisition detachments were formed to confiscate the products of other people's work. Peasants who grew crops and raised livestock had all, but a small portion taken from them. All the confiscated food was taken to the central administration and distributed to those who agreed to work for the communists, participate in their administration and support their system of repression, especially to the members of the Cheka – the Special Commission.

On June 2, 1918, a decree was issued stating that anyone found guilty of selling or storing food items monopolized by the Republic would be sentenced to imprisonment for at least ten years, with forced labour and the confiscation of all their property. Then, on November 21, 1918, all domestic trade was effectively monopolized, private traders were labelled as 'speculators' and persecuted by the Cheka. The private market was replaced with a centralized system of food distribution, and ration cards were introduced in November 1918. The number of ration cards printed exceeded the actual population, leading to the emergence of a black market.

The redistribution system was highly unequal. Workers in military factories received around 24 pounds of flour, 1–4 pounds of grain, 1–2 pounds of sugar, and 3–6 pounds of meat per month. Those considered former 'exploiters' received nothing but 50 to 250 grams of bread per day. Obtaining ration cards for those who were not civil servants, workers, soldiers, or lacked connections was often impossible. As a result, many people starved to death, especially during the winter and spring of 1919 when the daily bread ration in St Petersburg and Moscow was reduced to meagre 50–100 grams.

Many people were desperate to obtain food and firewood to heat their homes, so they turned to the communists and were willing to take on any job, just to secure some bread for their families. In this way, they also gained access to requisitioned products, becoming part of the communist system and implicitly committing crimes under the Russian law. Despite seeing their friends, relatives, and neighbours starve, they began to support the communists.

Because of malnutrition epidemics spread rapidly. During the civil war, approximately 9,000,000 people are believed to have lost their lives not due to military actions, but as a result of famine and the ensuing diseases.

But the parts of Russia that were not controlled by the Communists – Ukraine, Siberia, Finland or even the province of Arkhangelsk – were a world of food abundance and comfort – no one suffered from exhaustion there, public services were functioning, although life during the civil war was certainly not easy. This contrast proves that the famine in the regions under Bolshevik rule was not a result of a natural disaster or economic mistakes. After all, mistakes could easily be corrected by buying food from the peasants, since there was plenty of looted gold in the treasury. It was a deliberate policy.

How could the Bolsheviks create such a large-scale system of repression and property requisition? They set up Red Army detachments manned by native Latvians and Estonians. Despite their limited knowledge of the Russian language, the soldiers had strong financial incentives to support the Communists. The Bolsheviks had amassed substantial amounts of gold, which they used to pay these mercenaries, giving them the green light to act as they pleased. Financial gain, rather than ideological commitment, was their primary motivation. After the civil war, some of them returned to their homeland, where they bought land and lived as wealthy farmers. Others chose to continue their careers in Communist Russia.

The Bolsheviks succeeded in building a country where the majority were impoverished while a minority, including the communist leaders, enjoyed privileges and property. Those who opposed this system joined the White Army and fought against the

Bolsheviks. They didn't necessarily want to return to the pre-communist era, but rather to build a new Russia, a liberal or even socialist one. The first anti-communist governments of the Whites were socialist, but not communist in their nature. However, the majority of the population did not support them because the Whites wanted to restore the rule of law and respect for private property rights.

The initial success of the White Anti-Communist Resistance was facilitated by the collapse of the German and Austrian empires. Germany and Austria had supported the Bolsheviks, but after their defeat in November 1918, their troops, as well as Turkish troops, withdrew from Russia, leaving the Bolsheviks alone. Capitalizing on this, the Whites, backed by the Entente Powers, namely Great Britain, the United States, Japan and France, launched an offensive towards Moscow. By autumn 1919, they had regained control of approximately two thirds of the territory of the Russian Empire.

However, even in the liberated regions where anti-Communist administrations were established, the majority of the population did not support the Whites and were reluctant to fight in their ranks. Remember that the communist regime made people collaborate, forcing them to take the property that didn't belong to them. The Whites wanted to restore the rule of law, and this posed a threat to those who had received property and land from the Reds, i.e. the Bolsheviks. These people rightly feared that should the anti-communist forces win, their possessions would be confiscated, and they could potentially face legal persecution. They were afraid. As a result, more and more people saw the Whites as their enemies.

After five years of fighting, the White armies finally left Russia in November 1922. They had withdrawn from the European part of the country in November 1920 and from the Far East in November 1922. The country found itself under the firm grip of Communist dictatorship. Over a million people, mainly well-educated professionals and members of the old cultural and political elite, chose to go abroad. More than 12 million died in the civil war. Those who were considered part of the 'former exploiting classes' were deprived of almost all means of subsistence and suffered particularly badly, either falling victim to the Bolsheviks' Red Terror or succumbing to famine and epidemics.

Food rations were distributed according to one's social class, and scientists fell into the 'fourth category', receiving meagre leftovers. As a result, between 1918 and 1920, 22 full and associate members of the Academy of Sciences died of starvation, including mathematician Andrey Markov, philologist Alexey Shakhmatov, historian Alexander Lappo-Danilevsky, ethnographer Vasily Radlov, archaeologist Yakov Smirnov and world-famous Egyptologist Boris Turaev. Shortly before his death on 23 July 1920, Academician Turaev, who had devoted his entire life to study of the history and culture of the ancient Orient, told his close friends: 'There is no point in living if your soul is taken away, your spirit is crushed and all you have left is your stomach.' Many Russian cultural figures who held similar beliefs were either died or emigrated. The younger ones joined the White Movement, and many met their fate in Bolshevik prisons, such as the

Russian poet Nikolai Gumilev and the Moscow statesman Nikolai Shchepkin, both tortured to death. I first heard about the latter from Richard Pipes. To my shame, this hero of the anti-communist struggle had been unknown to me.

Almost nine tenth of Russia's relatively small cultural elite disappeared: some were killed, some died of unbearable living conditions, others emigrated. The loss is still felt today.

But the Communists were not only engaged in confiscating property and appropriating the fruits of labour. Their repressions went far beyond that. Another of their shocking practices was the 'Red Terror'. Not only the 'enemies of the regime' were targeted, Bolsheviks' goal was to instil fear, so they killed indiscriminately. More than 2,300,000 people lost their lives. Often their deaths were the result of horrific torture, and their mutilated bodies were sometimes displayed in public as a means of intimidation. This was the essence of the Bolshevik terror.

When the civil war ended and the communists prevailed, they had to face the harsh reality of a devastated nation. Russia lay in ruins and its economy in shambles, millions of lives were lost. Property requisitions had severely undermined the willingness of the population to engage in productive work. Faced with this sobering situation, the communists recognized the imperative for a change. In 1921, having consolidated their power in European Russia and subjected its population to a man-made famine, they introduced the New Economic Policy (NEP). It signalled a return to normal market principles, as running the country through repression alone was unsustainable.

Bolsheviks' ambitions extended far beyond Russian national borders. They never thought of themselves as mere Russian revolutionaries but were dreaming of a global domination. That's why they liked to call themselves 'internationalists' by the way. Soon after coming to power, in 1918–1919, they started to stir discord abroad.

In early 1918 they first tried to seize power in Finland, then the following year made similar attempts in Hungary, in Bavaria and various parts of Germany. Extending their reach even further, the Bolsheviks sought to take control of Iran, which led to the establishment of the Republic of Gilan south of the Caspian Sea in 1920. While their efforts to subjugate Estonia, Latvia, and Lithuania proved unsuccessful, they managed to establish control over the independent states of Azerbaijan, Armenia, and finally, Georgia in February and March 1921. In 1920 the Bolsheviks launched an offensive against Poland. Tukhachevsky, on Trotsky's orders, was tasked with advancing through Warsaw to Berlin. From the very outset of Bolshevik rule, their aim was to build a global communist empire and challenge the existing international order, 'to test the solidity of the capitalist world with a bayonet', as they put it.

But their efforts proved in vain. In August 1920, Polish army forced the Bolsheviks to retreat in the famous battle known as the Miracle on the Vistula. Despite this military setback the regime in Russia remained unchanged, as the majority of the population still clung to communist illusions.

Probably, as the New Economic Policy gathered pace, those illusions gradually started to fade away. People regained ownership of some property; money was brought back into circulation once again. One new rouble was exchanged for 50 billion old ones from 1918 to 1921. The economy began to recover. By 1927, both industry and agriculture in Russia had almost returned to their pre-war levels of 1913. People were quickly overcoming the turmoil of the revolution and beginning to rebuild their lives. But the Communists were well aware that the emergence of independent social groups with their own sources of income was a threat to their authoritarian regime. Self-sufficient peasants and workers could potentially demand political rights, and indeed the communists began to feel the pressure in some local elections. Since they claimed to represent the peasants and workers themselves, such trends signalled a potential erosion of the communists' grip on power.

The Bolsheviks never hid the fact that the economic liberalization was only a tactical manoeuvre, it was not permanent. It was not a change of political strategy, but a temporary measure to consolidate power. The main task of the Bolsheviks was not the prosperity of the people, but only power and all the privileges that came with it.

And indeed, the mask of the New Economic Policy was soon thrown off. In September and December 1927, at two meetings of the Communist leaders of Russia, Stalin announced a change in policy towards the peasantry. He argued that it was necessary to replace independent peasants with collective farms, independent in name, but de facto owned by the state. This new approach commonly known as 'collectivization' began in the second half of 1928.

Until then, under the new economic policy, peasants could sell their produce and earn a steady income. They paid taxes, invested in their businesses and spent the remaining money on their personal needs. In fact, the only thing they wanted from the state was to be allowed to live according to their own wishes. It's not surprising that they resisted collectivization.

Free and independent farming on one's own land was the core concept of the new economic policy, and the peasants were determined to maintain and even defend this way of life. But the communist leaders, Stalin, Bukharin, Rykov and Trotsky, understood only too well that granting land to the peasants and allowing them full and unrestricted use of the fruits of their labour would undermine the very basis of the communist dictatorship. Sensing a potential threat to their own power, they began the process of collectivization.

In 1927, when the Bolsheviks cut the state's purchase prices while increasing compulsory sales of agricultural products, peasants across the country refused to sell their grain to the state at the new reduced rate. Even in Siberia, where Stalin travelled personally to collect the grain, the peasants openly mocked him.

Stalin's reaction was swift and severe. The decision of the XV Party Congress in December 1927 read as follows: '[We should] intensify our offensive against the kulaks (i.e.

the rich peasants) and adopt a series of new measures to limit the development of capitalism in the countryside and to redirect the peasants towards socialism'. This meant banning the peasants from owning land and reducing them to agricultural labourers on Bolshevik-controlled plantations. For the sake of survival, these workers would quickly forget their human dignity and lose their freedom of enterprise.

When 'total collectivization' was announced in 1930, peasant uprisings broke out across the country. In Ukraine, the Don, Kuban, Terek, Western Siberia and parts of the Central Black Earth region, fierce fighting broke out between insurgents and paramilitary formations linked to the Bolshevik Party, reinforced by combined units of the Red Army. According to available data, between January and April 1930 staggering 6,117 peasant uprisings took place in Bolshevik-controlled territory of the USSR, involving an estimated 1.8 million people. However, the balance of power was heavily skewed. Over the course of the next six years, the Communists succeeded in effectively forcing almost all peasants living in the areas they controlled – from Belarus and Ukraine to the Transcaucasia, the Far East and Central Asia – to join collective and state farms.

Collectivization stands out as one of the most devastating events in twentieth-century Russia. Of course, its awful consequences were felt throughout the Soviet Union, in Ukraine, Belarus, Central Asian and Transcaucasian states. Some have compared it to the Holocaust. In order to force peasants to give up their property the state deliberately orchestrated three terrible famines. The first, known as the Volga famine, took place in 1921–1922 and spread from the Volga region to the most prosperous parts of Russia. The second occurred in 1932–1933 and the third after the World War II in 1946–1947.

All three were horrific, with reports of cannibalism from different parts of the country. The level of cruelty demonstrated by the Bolsheviks is appalling. They had the means and resources to alleviate suffering and prevent millions of deaths, but they were unswerving in their determination to starve the peasants into submission. In November 1932 they confiscated the entire harvest. As a result, at least six and a half million people starved to death over the following winter. Of course, the Bolsheviks understood the consequences of their actions, but they went ahead anyway and left a lot of documented evidence of their cruelty. While not all the archives in Russia have been fully opened, those in Ukraine and Kazakhstan have shed light on the well-organized system of mass extermination.

The aim of the famine was not to wipe out particular ethnic groups, such as Ukrainians or Kazakhs, nor to exterminate all the peasants. The Bolsheviks had another intention: to subjugate the free farmers and herders and turn them into obedient servants of the government. As in the years of the Red Terror (1918–1921), they wanted to deliberately kill some in order to instil fear and impose their control on the whole population. A tactic similar to the Roman military punishment of decimation, but on a national scale. Regions where resistance to collectivization was strongest, experienced the worst famines. In Ukraine, for example, some 4 million people died, while in

Kazakhstan, where free nomads refused to hand over their livestock to the Bolsheviks, nearly 1.5 million people lost their lives.

Overall, between 1930 and 1933, there were up to 9.3 million 'excess deaths' compared to the years of the NEP (1923–1926)[21]. Collectivization in general, and famine in particular, can rightly be described as another act of Bolshevik terror against the people.

When British Prime Minister Winston Churchill, a renowned expert on Russia, first met Stalin in mid-August 1942, he asked him about collectivization:

> *'Tell me,' I asked, 'have the stresses of this war been as bad to you personally as carrying through the policy of the Collective Farms?'*
> *This subject immediately roused the Marshal.*
> *'Oh, no,' he said, 'the Collective Farm policy was a terrible struggle.'*
> *'I thought you would have found it bad,' said I, 'because you were [...] dealing with [...] millions of small men.'*
> *'Ten millions,' he said, holding up his hands. 'It was fearful. Four years it lasted. [...]*
> *'These were what you call Kulaks?'*
> *'Yes,' he said, but he did not repeat the word. After a pause, 'It was all very bad and difficult – but necessary. [...] [T]he great bulk were very unpopular and were wiped out by their labourers.' [...]*
> *I did not repeat Burke's dictum, 'If I cannot have reform without injustice, I will not have reform.' With the World War going on all round us it seemed vain to moralise aloud*[22].

Churchill is choosing his words very carefully, but his account is corroborated by a secret stenographer's note of the meeting, taken by Stalin's secretary who was sitting in the adjoining room. Stalin did say that collectivization was the worst moment of his life. But when that book was translated into Russian and published in the Soviet Union (although for restricted use), this particular fragment was omitted.

The process of collectivization had very significant consequences, as it permanently dismantled Russia's traditional social structure. A predominantly agrarian nation effectively became a society of slaves.

You may recall that Peter the Great wanted Russia to be one of the dominant European powers. Before his reign, his siblings Sophia and Fyodor had tried to modernize Russia gradually, drawing inspiration from certain Polish practices. But Peter was impatient and wanted to make Russia great at once. To finance his ambitious plans for a large navy and army, he effectively enslaved the majority of the population and

---

21   According to the census held in January 1937, between 1926 and 1937 the population decreased by 5–18% in the following regions: Kalinin, West Region, Mordovia, Kursk, Caucasus, Volga German settlements, Saratov, Vinnytsia, Kyiv, Chernigov, Odessa and Kazakhstan. In the USSR as a whole, the population increased by 10%. See Е. М. Андреев, Л. Е. Дарский и Т. Л. Харькова, *Население Советского Союза: 1922–1991* (Москва: Наука, 1993). с. 118.

22   Winston Churchill, *The Second World War: Volume IV* (Boston: Houghton, Mifflin Company, 1950), pp. 447–448.

stripped them of their rights. His goal was achieved. With Peter in power, Russia emerged victorious from the Great Northern War and became an empire in 1721. But his brutal methods led to Russia's ultimate downfall in the flames of revolution two centuries later.

In the twentieth century, the situation was arguably similar. Russia had been a peasant country, slowly developing thanks to the New Economic Policy. Stalin wanted to turn it into a military superpower capable of conquering the world, or at least parts of Europe. This period coincided with the rise of fascist regimes in Italy and the growing influence of the Nazis in Germany. Stalin recognized the need to prepare for an impending major war, and he understood that the peasants living off their small farms would not provide him with sufficient resources to build a formidable military. Consequently, he made a rather ill-advised decision to return the Russian population to a state of serfdom. In this way, he tried to consolidate power in his own hands and extract resources from the population to support the military industry.

The cost of collectivization and the Holodomor was devastating. An estimated 9 million people lost their lives and a further 152 million domestic animals, including cows, horses and various other livestock, perished. It was an immense and tragic loss. Despite these sacrifices, Stalin's aims were not fully achieved.

The villages were destroyed and depopulated. As in 1921–1922, the West was ready to help starving Russia, although it had less capacity to do so because of the Great Depression. But the Bolsheviks were now reluctant to accept external help, and even the aid that did arrive rarely reached the dying peasants.

On the other hand, Western nations desperately needed markets for their products, and the Bolsheviks were eager to buy equipment and technology. That's why many in the West preferred to turn a blind eye to Stalin's atrocities. Numerous factories were built to produce all kinds of military equipment, from tanks to aeroplanes. However, as we will soon discover, these efforts had little positive effect.

One aspect in which Stalin did seem to succeed was in neutralizing the threat to Communist power posed by an independent peasantry: he simply wiped out any remnants of free entrepreneurial spirit. Half-starved peasants, whether actually working on state land or pretending to do so, could not object when they were asked to hand over all their cattle and grain to the state. The consolidation of power by the Communist elite seemed secure. But it did not take them long to discover that the people still had the resilience to resist.

In the wake of the terrible repressions of the early 1930s, Stalin turned his efforts to combating religion. Atheism became one of the core principles of his policy. The explanation is simple: people with religious ideals have a sense of independence. For independence can also come from religious conviction, from the unshakeable belief that something is greater than the rulers of this world, than 'the prince of the power of the air' [Eph 2:2]. It was these principles that provoked the Communist reaction. Their totalitarian ideology sought absolute control over every aspect of human life, both physical and spiritual, as only a totally subjugated person can be moulded into a soldier ready to fight for a global communist empire. Stalin believed that religion in Russia was almost eradicated, and the entire population of Russia was under his direct control. The anti-religious campaign had lasted for almost two decades, religious leaders had been persecuted, monasteries, churches, mosques and synagogues were either closed or destroyed. Deprived of faith, land and possessions, the Russian people had been reduced to a mere silent mass with no meaning in life beyond their physical survival.

Once the peasants had been forced into collective farms, Stalin began to think about a constitution for the Soviet State. The concept of a fundamental law had been among the most progressive ideas in previous centuries. By the early 20th century most of the countries had such texts, inspired by the examples of France, Poland and the United States. Stalin organized a nationwide referendum (the results of which were obviously manipulated anyway), and on 5 December 1936, the Soviet Constitution was adopted. This was a very special document. It gave people all sorts of freedoms, including freedom of speech, freedom of belief, freedom of economic activity. The only problem was that its ideas were never put into practice and remained a dead letter forever.

Immediately afterwards, communists started preparation for a new census, to understand the size of the population, people's beliefs and activities. It took place on 7 January 1937, coinciding with Russian Orthodox Christmas. One of the questions was added to the census form by Stalin himself: it was about one's attitude to religion. Never before have such questions been asked by the Communists. The accompanying instructions were quite clear: 'This question should only be answered by individuals aged 16 and over. It does not refer to any religion officially practised in the past by the respondents or their parents. If the respondent identifies as a non-believer, write "non-believer". If the respondent identifies as a believer, write "believer". For believers who belong to a specific faith, indicate the name of the religion.'[23]

Interestingly, only those older than sixteen were asked about their religious affiliations during the census. The question was not about traditional, family religious practices, but rather about their own personal faith. Of course, questionnaires were not anonymous, as full name and all personal details were also recorded. In such a context, an honest answer about one's religion became an open and defiant declaration of one's own creed.

The census showed that the population of Russia was smaller than expected. Experts in the Soviet Statistics Department estimated that the Soviet Union had a population of 180 million people. The actual figure was 162 million, a difference of 18 million. This difference could be attributed to collectivization and other horrific population massacres.

---

23 В.Б.Жиромская, Ю.А.Поляков (Сост.), *Всесоюзная перепись населения. 1937. Общие итоги. Сборник документов и материалов* (Москва: РОССПЭН, 2007).

The second notable finding was that 56.7% of the population over the age of sixteen identified themselves as believers. The majority of them were Orthodox Christians, but about 13% were Muslims, Jews and followers of other religions. It's quite extraordinary that in the terrible year of 1937, after two decades of Communist rule, the majority of the Russians had the courage to openly express their religious beliefs. It is impossible to determine the exact number of people who chose to hide their true convictions or gave false answers. Nevertheless, 56.7% of the population, or 55.3 million people, openly spoke of their faith in an atheistic, totalitarian and repressive state. I think this is an unparalleled act of non-conformism in the twentieth century in the whole world.

Upon learning of the results of the census, Stalin and the Politburo went to great lengths to keep its findings secret, including destroying the census documents and even executing the sociologists involved in it. Despite their efforts, however, some fragments of the documented evidence survived. After the end of the communist era, painstaking research in archives allowed us to uncover certain elements and we have since published everything we could find. The results of this census are of great value, but their immediate consequences were devastating.

On 20 May 1937, Malenkov, a member of the Politburo who would later briefly rule the USSR between Stalin's death and Khrushchev's rise to power, wrote an internal memorandum to Stalin. In this memo he explained that it would be impossible to liberate the world from the bourgeoisie (i.e. to achieve global domination) given the existing public sentiment. He proposed purging the Soviet Union of dissidents and religious nonconformists. On May 26, the Politburo met to discuss the matter, and on 2 July 1937 it was decided to launch large-scale repressions to get rid of believers, nonconformists and anyone considered anti-Communist. On 13 July 1937, the People's Commissariat for Internal Affairs (NKVD) issued the secret decree 00447, which marked the beginning of the Great Terror.

The consequences of the Great Terror are best reflected in the official figures: 1,575,000 people were arrested, of whom 681,000 were killed within just fifteen months. I am sure, however, that the real figures are much higher. I had the opportunity to meet Alexander Yakovlev, a remarkable figure and strong supporter of Gorbachev, who served in the Politburo during perestroika and worked personally in the archives. He believed that the true figures were much higher than the official ones. The wave of repression targeted not only the general population but also high-ranking Communist officials, including members of the Politburo. Shockingly, some of those who had signed the document launching the Great Terror in July 1937 became its victims in the months that followed. Namely, Yagoda and Yezhov, who successively served as heads of the NKVD. Violence permeated the military. Stalin, preparing for a potential conflict with Europe, ordered the execution of half of his generals and admirals, fearing that they might seize power from him.

It is important to remember that the Soviet elite's primary objective was power. National ideals, socialist principles, elaborate ideologies inspired by Marx or Hegel played a secondary role. Pursuit of a global communist state was a mere fiction. The lust for power and the fear of losing it were their main and only driving force. Everything else was just propaganda.

As history has repeatedly shown, the ultimate test for a state is war, as we are witnessing now with the ongoing conflict between Russia and Ukraine. In times of war, the clouds of propaganda dissipate, and reality is revealed. The devastating war that broke out in 1939 exposed a simple truth: the Communist state and its army were deeply flawed. They proved ineffective even in their battles with the Finnish army in 1939–1940. The regime that seemed so formidable turned out to have feet of clay. The communists could instil fear and carry out massacres, but they lacked strength in other essential aspects. The Bolsheviks' relentless pursuit of power resulted in a weakened and ailing state.

On 29 November 1939, Stalin attacked Finland, believing that its defeat would be no big deal. He even gave the order to set up a puppet Communist government for the future 'Democratic Republic of Finland', led by his protégé, Otto Wille Kuusinen. His ambitions were never realized. The Finnish people, under the political leadership of Risto Ryti's government and the military command of Baron Carl Gustav Mannerheim, resisted Soviet aggression and remained unconquered. In March 1940, Stalin was forced to sign a peace treaty in Moscow with the 'bourgeois' Finnish state. Three million Finns successfully defended their borders against the mighty Soviet Union of 170 million people, inflicting heavy losses on it. This is the result of the first 22 years of Bolshevik rule in Russia.

Coming to terms with Bolshevism

In this lecture we will focus on a long period, from the World War II to Perestroika. Obviously, it's impossible to cover all the details, so we'll try to narrow down our discussion to a few specific points instead. The overarching theme of the previous lecture was the building of a global totalitarian state by the Communist regime. I'll try to avoid using the term 'communist', as it's misleading and carries a lot of ideological connotations that had little to do with the administration in Russia. Instead, most of the time I'll use the term 'Bolshevism' to get rid of any unnecessary semantics that might cloud our understanding. The Bolsheviks were masters at spreading all sorts of falsehoods and lies. For example, they called their country the Union of Soviet Socialist Republics, which is completely inaccurate. A Soviet is a council elected by the workers and peasants, and this was true in 1917. By mid-1918, however, the soviets were merely a façade for the totalitarian regime. In fact, the term 'sovietize' was used to imply the approval of a decision of the party organs by the soviets in order to give it a veneer of legitimacy. It was, of course, inconceivable for a Soviet to reject such a decision. They became nothing more than a symbol of totalitarian dictatorship.

It is important to get our terminology right. Confucius, the ancient Chinese philosopher, when asked where to begin reform, replied, 'Start by rectifying names.' [Lun Yu 13.3]. Why? Because wrong names need to be replaced with right ones. Otherwise we won't be able to understand what's really going on and how to correct our mistakes. We are so used to talking about a communist dictatorship, a communist state or a communist ideology that we often fail to see that the word 'communist' in this context is just a deceptive label. Communism implies public ownership of all resources, which never really existed under Bolshevik rule. Instead, resources were controlled by a tiny elite, perhaps no more than twelve people. At times, such as during the Stalin era, it was the rule of a single person, while at other times there were variations such as triumvirates or duumvirates. So, if we want to be accurate and follow Confucius's principles, this regime can best be described as the totalitarian rule of a gang with no electoral mandate and no regard for the law or public opinion.

The same can be said of the term 'socialist'. Socialism is about public ownership, i.e. a form of political organization in which property is managed collectively rather than individually. I personally have doubts that such a system can even exist. A social state, that is, a state that acts in the interests of all members of society and supports the poor and the weak using the resources of the rich and the strong, is of course possible, but it is not socialism. In any case, socialism should be inseparable from democracy, because property must be managed by the society through freely elected representatives. Nothing of the sort ever existed in Russia under the Bolsheviks. Confiscated property was disposed of by appointed bureaucrats who were accountable only to the Bolshevik leaders who had seized power in the country by force. The term 'socialist' had no meaning for them, it was nothing more than empty rhetoric using Marxist language. They could just as easily have called themselves liberals, Christians or even extraterrestrials without any significant change in their actions or policies.

Nor was the USSR a republic, since a republic is governed by representative institutions elected by its citizens (hence the Latin term 'res publica', meaning 'public affair'). In Bolshevik Russia, however, there were neither elections nor representative institutions. The country was under the control of a small group of criminals who had seized power, called themselves socialists and used a system of co-optation to recruit new members of their gang as old ones fell away. This regime of recruitment and power transfer makes them look very much alike Chicago gangsters or Cosa Nostra.

There was no union in the sense of a voluntary association of peoples and territories. Instead, there existed a regime of ruthless coercion that forced obedience on all individuals and communities living in the territories the Bolsheviks managed to subjugate. Initially confined to the historical territory of Russia, by the 1950s it had expanded to cover almost a third of the earth's surface, stretching from Indochina to Brandenburg and from the Arctic Circle to the Caribbean islands. The insatiable appetite of the Bolshevik gang knew no bounds.

Therefore, all four words in the name of the 'Union of Soviet Socialist Republics' were utter falsehoods, deliberately chosen to deceive the enslaved population and to manipulate the so-called useful idiots living in still free societies.

As you can see from the above, it's no exaggeration to say that the regime that took root in Russia after the civil war of 1917–1922 was essentially that of a mafia-like gang. And while we may occasionally call them 'communists', let us not deceive ourselves. There was no trace of communist ideology left.

The Bolsheviks had two main aims. First, their leaders sought personal power, control over individuals. And second, they wanted to extend their rule to the rest of the world. They dreamed of global hegemony, although they were not particularly successful in achieving this in the early decades of their rule. As you may recall, Lenin had tried and failed to annex Poland and Germany in 1920. Stalin, in his turn, renewed attempts at territorial expansion. After 1929, he set about building a formidable military force capable of invading countries not yet under Communist control.

It all seemed to play into Stalin's hands, because at the same time Adolf Hitler was coming to power in Germany. Driven by dreams of revenge, he set out to rebuild the Reich that Germany had lost after World War I. He sought to reclaim the territories taken from Germany under the Treaty of Versailles and harboured secret thoughts of further expansion. Hitler concentrated on uniting the German-speaking countries, but he was also thinking of providing the great German nation with Lebensraum, a living space, in the East, especially in Russia.

Stalin had his own cunning plan. It was quite simple, yet treacherous. He intended to provoke Germany into wars against Poland and Czechoslovakia. Stalin knew that the former Entente countries, namely France and Great Britain, would come to the aid of the Poles and Czechs, triggering a new major conflict in Europe. As in the World War I, both sides would suffer heavy casualties. Meanwhile, Stalin would remain a 'third rejoicing', appearing neutral and taking advantage of the power shifts. As the war draws to a close, Stalin would launch his invasion of Europe. Given the exhaustion of Germany, France and Britain after years of warfare, he would easily 'liberate' them from 'bourgeois' oppression'. In this way, Stalin intended to enlarge his empire, encompassing the whole of Europe, and perhaps even extending his rule worldwide.

Many in Bolshevik Russia also supported this criminal expansionism. Pavel Kogan, a young poet, expressed his feelings in his verses in 1940: 'I am a devoted patriot of the Russian land and sky, even if it may seem narrow-minded to some. We are determined to march to the Ganges, to die in battles, so that our motherland may shine from Japan to England.'

Stalin wanted Hitler to initiate the war, so encouraged him as he could. When the Munich Agreement was concluded, resulting in the dismemberment of Czechoslovakia, Stalin didn't mind. In fact, he was quite happy that Hitler had been given control over that country, as it provided a good starting ground for German aggression in the West.

On the other hand, Hitler was certain that if he were to attack Poland, he would have to face opposition from Great Britain and France, and potentially from the Soviet Union who had similar security arrangements with Warsaw. However, on the 23rd of August 1939, the Molotov-Ribbentrop Pact was signed in Moscow. Not only it gave Hitler a free hand to start his aggression against Poland but also created new borders between the two empires in the Baltic region, Poland, Finland, and even Romania.

Before signing the pact, on August 19, Stalin held a meeting with other Bolshevik strongmen. All the related documents are still classified, but we have some leaked testimony. Apparently, Stalin had made a speech about the need to play Western countries off against each other, without direct USSR involvement. His strategy was to wait until the West was exhausted.

Hitler, for his part, was ecstatic and seemed rather naive in his reading of Stalin's intentions. 'The whole world is now in my pocket!' he is reported to have exclaimed to his generals. Hitler was likely unaware of the true strength of the Russian army, which largely surpassed German forces at that time. By the end of August 1939, Germany possessed 52.5 divisions, while Russia boasted 147. Germany had 30,600 artillery guns, while Russia had 55,800. Germany had 3,400 tanks, whereas Russia had 21,000. Furthermore, Germany had 4,300 military aircraft, while Russia had 11,000.

Stalin tried to limit the use of military force, and he managed to occupy his part of Poland without giving much of a fight. He then occupied the Baltic States, but, as you remember, he met with stubborn resistance in Finland. The Finns refused to sign any agreements with the USSR and the Winter War began. It was the Winter War that somehow changed Hitler's thinking. He realized that the Russian army was indeed very large, although not very strong.

This revelation was deeply unsettling also for Stalin. It became apparent that the strength of the Red Army was compromised. Even a relatively small Finnish army successfully resisted the Soviet Forces during more than a hundred days. The main underlying reason was the poor level of education of the Communist officers and generals compared to their Finnish and German counterparts. A significant number of experienced Bolshevik commanders had been purged from the army just before the war by Stalin himself. Furthermore, the soldiers, predominantly former peasants who had survived collectivization violence, harboured a deep-seated resentment towards the communist regime. Their feelings were evident in the 1937 general census, where the majority declared their religious beliefs, openly defying the atheistic and repressive Bolshevik regime.

Stalin was not opposed to a war on the Western Front between Germany and France and Britain, but he had expected the military action to be longer and more exhausting. To his dismay, the German army managed to quickly defeat the French and British forces in just five weeks, from May to June 1940. Stalin began to fear that the Germany was much stronger than he had expected, while his own forces were not as formidable as he had hoped. Consequently, he decided to avoid starting a war, although he was well aware that Hitler was considering an attack on the Soviet Union after his failure in the Battle of Britain. Stalin was secretly preparing for a conflict with Germany and had discussed a possible preventive war with his generals and close associates. This war, he planned, was to be fought in Europe, outside the borders of the Soviet Union. We now know that the date chosen for this offensive was 12 July 1941.

Hitler was aware of Stalin's plans and initially intended to launch an attack on Russia on 15 May 1941. However, his focus shifted when a pro-British coup took place in Serbia in May. Hitler had to focus on crushing Serbia and Greece before turning his attention to Russia. As a result, he lost valuable time, about five weeks of warm spring weather, before starting his offensive on June 22. This conflict once again exposed the weaknesses of the Red Army to the whole world. The Soviet Union had more planes, tanks and guns than the Germans, and was only outnumbered in manpower on the Eastern Front by a factor of 1.3 (there were approximately 1.3 German soldiers for every Russian soldier). But sheer numbers did not translate into technical superiority. Soviet military personnel lacked proper training and expertise. As a result, the Red Army suffered significant defeats in the early months of the war and was forced to retreat, allowing the enemy to advance dangerously close to Moscow.

During the World War I, the German army had never advanced beyond the western regions of Ukraine, Belarus and the Baltic provinces. Riga, for example, had not been taken until September 1917. This time, however, in 1941, within a week of the outbreak of war, on July 1, the Nazis were in control of Riga, and within a month and a half they had occupied much of Ukraine, Belarus and the Baltic region. Once again the Bolsheviks discovered that their strength was not as unassailable as they believed. The majority of the population paid little attention to the ideological gibberish and were unwilling to sacrifice their lives for the regime. Over three and a half million of Russian soldiers chose not to fight and surrendered in the early months of the war. Dedicated Bolshevik imperialists, such as the above-mentioned poet Pavel Kogan, were a tiny minority. Tragically, Pavel himself, aged 22 at the start of the war, was killed in action near Novorossiysk in September 1942.

A significant shift took place in the second half of 1942 and was felt worldwide. At the beginning of the year, the prevailing belief was that Germany and its allies would prevail. Many toyed with the idea of a peace treaty between the aggressors and their victims. In the second half of 1942, however, three key events took place. First, the Battle of Midway (4–7 June 1942) between the Japanese and US navies resulted in a resounding victory for the United States. Secondly, the Battle of El Alamein (October-November 1942), where the British Army triumphed over the German and Italian forces. Finally, the Battle of Stalingrad (July 1942-January 1943), where the Nazis and their allies suffered a crushing defeat. These three battles marked the beginning of a turning point.

Crucially, the public mood in Russia changed. The Russian people finally realized that they were fighting not just for the Bolshevik regime, but for their lives, their homes and their future. They were fighting not for Stalin, but for themselves.

Grigory Pomerants, a young volunteer soldier who fought at Stalingrad and many years later became a famous philosopher, recalled: 'The outcome of the war was decided by those (mostly killed) soldiers, sergeants and officers who stood their ground, even though those to their right and left were fleeing... By one's faith in the nearest commander ... and that commander's ability to lead in close combat. A strategic plan? It only made sense because Stalingrad stood strong. In Stalingrad, the commanders had no communication with the units, the battalions held their positions on their own... It was the spirit of the soldiers and volunteers that proved decisive. Where it came from, this spirit, no one will ever fully explain... The war penetrated to the core of my being. I became a soldier, and in some moments I still feel like one. A lone warrior ... fighting his own battle... There have been many millions of such infinitesimal shifts... At the edge of the abyss, in the time of the plague, [the Russian soldier] proved to be different, not the one he was in times of peace...'. [24].

Following this shift in mindset, Russian soldiers were driven by a dual motivation. On the one hand, they wanted to crush the enemy; on the other, they wanted to change life at home after the war. They longed for an end to repression, the dismantling of collective farms and a return to a traditional peasant way of life. They dreamed of reopening closed churches and monasteries and establishing freely elected local governments.

When the war ended in 1945, Stalin had to deal with a nation that had deeply changed. Despite the devastating losses suffered by all countries involved in the conflict, the scale of suffering in the Soviet Union was immense. The numbers alone are staggering and not yet fully known – some 27 million killed and 56 million injured. Probably even more. But those who survived this harrowing experience emerged as new individuals, with a renewed sense of purpose and destiny. They longed to live in a free country, not the Bolshevik-controlled Soviet Union. They had no more faith in the State propaganda and wanted to concentrate on building their own lives, rather than on a worldwide communist empire or a proletarian brotherhood. Moreover, they had seen Europe and realized that ordinary people in the West enjoyed a higher standard of living. The Bolshevik lie had evaporated. These returning soldiers, and even civilian workers forced by the Nazis to work in Germany, shared those simple facts with their friends, spouses, children and neighbours. The realization that the Western world offered greater prosperity than the USSR spread even among Soviet officers, reaching the army generals. Suddenly the possibility of Stalin losing power seemed less far-fetched.

The Bolsheviks resorted to their usual methods of maintaining power. The first was terror, which reached alarming proportions after the war. Countless people were arrested en masse and sent to labour camps. Then there was starvation. The same tactics had been employed in the early 1930s to force peasants into collective farms. In 1946 almost all grain was confiscated. Despite the catastrophic situation that followed, Stalin refused to spare a single rouble to import food from abroad. Russia's post-war gold reserves were full, replenished by the plundering of Eastern European states under Soviet occupation, but Stalin withheld all support from his own people. The resulting famine was devastating, claiming some 1.4 million lives, both from starvation and the resulting epidemics. Furthermore, while Stalin reluctantly agreed to accept UN food

---

24   Григорий Померанц, *Записки гадкого утёнка* [*Notes of an Ugly Duckling*] (Москва: Московский рабочий, 1998), pp. 149–150.

aid for Ukraine and Belarus, he adamantly refused the same aid for Russia, fearing that UN commissioners would witness the extreme poverty of rural areas that had never been under Nazi occupation.

The Bolsheviks intensified and adapted their propaganda efforts. Before the World War II, their main message was one of global communist revolution. During the war, however, Stalin decided to revive Russian imperialist ideas. In September 1943 he reopened churches and allowed the practice of all religions, albeit under strict KGB control. He even reintroduced the old military uniform, but with gold-plated shoulder boards. The civil bureaucracy also adopted a pre-revolutionary style uniform. In 1946, Stalin changed the names of key ministries, such as the Ministry of Foreign Affairs, the Ministry of the Interior and so on. After the revolution, as suggested by Lev Trotsky, they used to be called 'people's commissariats'. In February 1946, the 'Red Army of Workers and Peasants' was renamed the 'Soviet Army', the name it retained until the end of the USSR.

Russian history was selectively used for propaganda purposes. The World War I and the deeds of influential figures such as Peter the Great and Catherine II were presented in a positive light and served as elements of Stalinist propaganda. This was not the case for Alexander I and Alexander II, tsars who thought about emancipation and freedom. The Bolsheviks persistently portrayed the anti-Bolshevik White movement in an intensely negative way. They saw them as their implacable opponents. The White generals were consistently called puppets of the Western powers, 'the lapdogs of the Entente'. On the other hand, the incorporation of various nations into the Russian Empire was now presented as a positive development. This wave of nationalist sentiment quickly took on anti-Semitic overtones. Indeed, the so-called fight against cosmopolitanism that began in the post-war years was primarily directed against the Jews.

Many Red Army officers and generals, as well as many Russians, remembered their imperial past and were ready to welcome Stalin as a national, not a communist, leader. There was even a period at the end of 1946 when he thought about restoring the monarchy and declaring himself tsar, and that's one of the reasons why he wanted the emigrants back so that they could embrace him as the legitimate successor to traditional Russian monarchy. But Stalin soon realized that this was a dead end, because the Communists who supported him as their leader would never support him as tsar. That's why, in September 1947, at a conference of Communist parties in Szklarska Poręba, Poland, the regime underwent a major face-lift. On the one hand, this meeting established Cominform, the Information Bureau of the Communist and Workers' Parties, an agency directed at the outside world. On the other hand, Stalin intensified internal propaganda, with particular emphasis on Russian nationalism, while still paying lip service to communism.

In parallel, after his triumph over the Nazis, Stalin started preparations for a new war against the Western world. Following the Berlin crisis of 1948–1949, even the nuclear option was seriously considered by the Kremlin. The outbreak of the Korean War in July 1950 further fuelled Stalin's ambitions and serious preparations for a major global conflict began. In January 1951, a secret meeting was held with the leaders of Czechoslovakia, Poland, Hungary, Bulgaria and Romania, along with their military generals and Stalin's inner circle. The official records are still classified, but fragments of information have leaked out through the recollections and memoirs of Eastern European leaders and military officials. It is known that they discussed plans for a new war in Europe, scheduled for early 1954 at the latest. There may have been other similar meetings to refine these plans, we don't know. Stalin clearly wanted to expand his empire beyond the eastern lands of Europe. To support these ambitions, huge shipbuilding facilities were built on the Pacific Ocean near Sovetskaya Havan (formerly Imperatorskaya Havan, Emperor's Harbour). The atomic project was personally overseen by Beria, Stalin's right-hand man: new design offices and factories were opened for the production of missiles, atomic bombs and jet aircraft. A staggering 90% of new investment after 1949 went to the military industry, while most of the population continued to live in misery.

People who had been arrested before the war and then released were re-arrested to stifle potential opposition, leading many to believe that a new wave of repression, similar to that of 1937, was underway. Members of the government did not escape the purges: even if Molotov, Kalinin or Alexander Poskrebyshev, Stalin's secretary, were not targeted directly, their wives were thrown into prisons and subjected to abuse and violence. This is one of the reasons why we believe that Stalin did not die of natural causes.

He died unexpectedly on 5 March 1953, leaving open the question of whether his death was somehow staged by his associates, who had been celebrating with him in his dacha in Kuntsevo on the night of February 28 to March 1. These are not just unfounded rumours, as the Kremlin elite were strongly opposed to another war and feared another round of internal violence. They were also well aware that such a confrontation would inevitably lead to nuclear devastation, annihilating not only the Soviet Union but potentially the entire world. Memories were still vivid of high-ranking civilian and military officials being arrested, subjected to inhuman torture and finally executed by a bullet to the back of the head. The 'Leningrad case' also showed that high rank in the communist party was no guarantee of safety. Naturally, those who had survived the horrors of 1937 had no desire to suffer the fate of their victims.

The death of Stalin brought immediate changes. The first post-Stalin government was controlled by Georgy Malenkov acting as Prime Minister, Lavrentiy Beria as his First Deputy and Head of the Ministry of the Interior, and Nikita Khrushchev as Leader of the Communist Party. They quickly ended the Korean War, which was threatening to escalate into a global conflict. When North Korean leader Kim Il-sung came to Moscow for Stalin's funeral on March 9, he was informed that the war should cease immediately.

Kim Il-sung was surprised, as was the Chinese leader Mao Zedong. But as the USSR was the strongest country within the communist bloc, they had to comply. The armistice was signed on 27 July 1953, bringing peace to the Korean peninsula.

Austria was granted neutral status, and in 1955 all occupying forces withdrew from its territory. Beria had thoughts about extending the same status to Germany, but these plans were not realized due to his arrest and execution in late 1953. So, Germany remained divided between the Communist German Democratic Republic and the Federal Republic of Germany. Nevertheless, Khrushchev made efforts to improve relations with West Germany, and by 1956 prisoners of war were able to return home. In addition, many ethnic groups, including the Chechens and Kalmyks (but the Crimean Tatars and Germans) who had been deported during the World War II, were permitted to return to their ancestral lands.

Khrushchev was the first Bolshevik leader to try to curb the omnipresent aggression. The early years of his rule were marked by the first attempts to foster better relations with Western Europe and the United States. In a significant departure from the past, his government took an interest in the well-being of ordinary people. Many Gulag prisoners were released, and a programme of low-cost housing construction was launched. This used to be a big issue, as many people had to live in cramped pre-revolutionary flats where each family occupied one room. I remember my father praising these achievements when he talked about Krushchev. He used to say that whatever reservations one might have about some of his other actions, people would be eternally grateful to him.

Perhaps one of Khrushchev's most significant initiatives was his campaign against Stalin's cult of personality. This may come as a surprise, considering his own involvement as one of Stalin's most ruthless henchmen. Nonetheless, at the 20th Congress of the Communist Party of the Soviet Union in February 1956, Khrushchev openly exposed and condemned Stalin's dark legacy. Despite facing staunch opposition from many party members who fiercely defended Stalin, monuments to the Soviet dictator were dismantled across the country, and in 1962 his body was removed from the mausoleum in Moscow's Red Square. Numerous high-ranking officials, responsible for the torture and murder of hundreds of thousands of Soviet citizens, were either imprisoned or executed. It is true that Khrushchev was probably not driven by a sudden desire to restore morality to politics. He did not hesitate to deploy tanks to crush the Hungarian uprising in the summer of 1956, and in June 1962 he ordered the shooting of peaceful demonstrators in Novocherkassk. For Khrushchev, condemning Stalin was a way of gaining the upper hand over his equally bloodstained rivals such as Molotov, Malenkov and Kaganovich.

Khrushchev tried to change the principles of Soviet administration, but he remained true to the idea of expanding the Bolshevik empire. He significantly reduced the size of the army and hoped to compete with the West economically, aiming to 'catch up and overtake America'. However, his efforts were ultimately in vain. Perhaps Khrushchev, poorly educated as he was, genuinely believed in the benefits of socialism, unaware that it was merely an ideological cover for the criminal regime. Towards the end of his rule, realizing the failure of peaceful competition with capitalism, he reverted to aggressive rhetoric and nuclear intimidation. Relations with the Western world deteriorated, culminating in the new Berlin crisis of 1961–1962, marked by the building of the Berlin Wall. A further escalation of the Cold War, the Cuban Missile Crisis in October 1962, brought the world once again dangerously close to nuclear conflict. Finally, in October 1964, Khrushchev was removed from office.

The new leader, Leonid Brezhnev, sought to maintain the stability of the regime and improve relations with the West. He didn't abandon the goal of expanding his empire, but he did so with greater caution. But his ambitions were thwarted by the events in Czechoslovakia in August 1968. It was during this period that the USSR's foreign policy, known as the 'Brezhnev Doctrine', was formulated. The principle was simple and straightforward: 'What is mine is mine, and we will still see what is yours.' Nevertheless, a major war was not considered a desirable option, as Brezhnev liked to be seen as a peacemaker.

In 1975, he signed the Helsinki Final Act, which aimed to establish fixed borders in Europe and promote further détente. The treaty also included humanitarian provisions, known as the 'third basket'. Despite these diplomatic efforts, Brezhnev continued to pursue the expansion of the Soviet empire whenever opportunities arose. One such opportunity came in Africa after the collapse of the Portuguese Empire in 1974. With the help of the Cuban Communist army, the USSR sought to gain control over Angola, Mozambique and other former Portuguese colonies. At the same time, relations with the Communist China were deteriorating. We all feared a possible confrontation between the two Communist powers. This may have contributed to Brezhnev's efforts to maintain positive relations with the West.

In 1979, the USSR sent its troops into Afghanistan, possibly without Brezhnev's personal approval. It was to be the Soviet Union's last military engagement, an aggressive and imperialist war that led to the loss of over a million Afghan lives.

Brezhnev passed away on 9 November 1982. After him, Andropov, then Chernenko, tried to maintain Bolshevik control over Russia. But it was clear that the totalitarian system was in decline. The communist state was not as strong as it had been, and economic challenges were evident. The war in Afghanistan was proving both unsuccessful and deeply unpopular. The unexpected election of Mikhail Gorbachev as the new leader at the spring meeting of the Communist Party in 1985 took everyone by surprise. No one knew what policies he would pursue.

I vividly remember the moment when Mikhail Gorbachev addressed the plenary session of the Communist Party. His words signalled the beginning of significant and positive changes that would reshape the life of our nation. For the first and only time in the history of Bolshevik Russia, a Russian leader spoke of the importance of universal human values overriding 'class values' and 'class goals'. Communist and Bolshevik ideology was fading. New principles of peaceful coexistence were proclaimed at a meeting with Ronald Reagan in Reykjavik in 1986 and with George H. W. Bush in Malta in 1989. Both the United States and the Soviet Union agreed to reduce their nuclear arsenals by 50%. The ideas of an empire, of a world communist state, of global domination, were a thing of the past. Mikhail Gorbachev was the architect of this transformation.

Indeed, foreign policy was only one side of the coin, but Gorbachev also tried to liberalize and open up Russian society. He was the first to speak about independent media and economic pluralism. Transformations in foreign policy are not sustainable when they are not accompanied by changes inside the country. Liberalism in international relations is a poor match to a repressive criminal order inside the country.

However, there was a major flaw in Gorbachev's thinking. He genuinely believed in Communist ideology in Lenin's interpretation. He constantly proclaimed the necessity to get 'back to Lenin' and to promote 'more socialism'. But a return to Lenin's principles would mean a new wave of red terror and property confiscation. Gorbachev's romantic understanding of Lenin is historically misguided. But his misreading of the social realities of the Soviet Union is even more so. Gorbachev sincerely believed that everyone lived in peace and friendship and that the apparent social stability was natural and not the result of oppressive control by the KGB. He was genuinely surprised when he found that reducing the level of control led to immediate ethnic conflicts between different groups, such as Azerbaijanis and Armenians, Abkhazians and Georgians, and a rise in tensions in Central Asia and Moldova involving the Russian-speaking population of Transnistria.

I remember these events quite well because I was already involved in politics at that time and had contacts with some of Gorbachev's close colleagues. He really didn't fully understand what was going on and didn't know what to do. But let's recall the beginning of our lecture and everything will become clear. A communist regime was a gang rule, and the only way to maintain unity within the gang is through terror. As soon as the level of repression falls, everything starts to crumble. A normal society is underpinned by countless horizontal connections. Even if we are not always aware of them, they are there. They permeate our lives and show themselves in self-government, private trade, elections, etc. The communist system destroyed them all. From the beginning, the Bolshevik leaders imposed a vertical axis of strict control, and seventy years later, they really succeeded in enforcing it. Russians forgot what a normal society was and how it was supposed to work.

Eastern European countries such as Czechoslovakia, Poland, Hungary and Bulgaria struggled to return to a normal way of life as well. For them, however, it was easier, because despite the broken links with the past, older people still remembered how they used to live. The younger generation relied on their stories to understand life before communism. In Russia, these historical connections completely disappeared. Gorbachev did not understand this. He believed that economic and political changes would make everything better. This was not the case.

While there were improvements in international relations, especially with the United States, Britain and other NATO allies, the domestic situation was dire. The events that followed were dramatic. In December 1991, Gorbachev lost power and the Soviet Union collapsed. The path to a more prosperous life was lost for years. The bright future ahead was just a mirage.

Breaking the cycle

In our previous lecture, we tried to uncover the nature of the Bolshevik regime. It's, of course, simplistic and naive to think of Stalin as a staunch Communist or a leader genuinely concerned with the welfare of the people. It was important to dispel romantic ideas about the intentions of the Bolsheviks and to show that they were essentially a criminal gang with no ideological basis. Sure, honesty was not Lenin's strong point, but he was certainly not lying when he supposedly said that those in the West who supported the Russian Bolsheviks out of personal Communist conviction were just 'useful idiots'.

Around that time, Vitaly Naishul, a 35-year-old economist who would later claim in the 2000s that he had invented the concept of privatization in 1981, wrote in 'Another Life', a book that was secretly distributed through samizdat channels:

'Give the property back to the people. All the country's enterprises, including shops, cafes, factories, plants, collective and state farms, garages and other forms of public property should really be in the hands of the people – in your hands and in ours.

Why can't we just hand over the companies to their directors, ministers and other high-ranking officials? Firstly, it would be unfair and unacceptable for a small group to claim ownership of the whole country; no one would agree to it. Secondly, concentrating property in the hands of a privileged few would lead to an economy that favoured the rich over ordinary workers. The October Revolution had equalized property, and we would never willingly return to a society of servants and masters again[25].'

Naishul, a researcher at the Central Institute of Economics and Mathematics, gave semi-legal lectures, which some of us had the opportunity to attend. But in his works, despite their markedly market-oriented inspirations, the idealization of Lenin's Bolshevism as true socialism remains evident.

25   V. A. Naishul, *Another Life [Drugaya Zhizn']* (Moscow: published in Samizdat, 1985).

Mikhail Gorbachev was arguably the first Soviet leader to genuinely embrace socialist values. Neither Khrushchev nor Brezhnev before him had taken them seriously. His wife Raisa shared the same views, and similar ideas were quite popular among Russian intellectuals at the time[26].

Gorbachev was pragmatic in his political agenda, but there was a certain naivety in his approach. I knew him quite well and we met many times after his resignation. He was sincere in his beliefs, and he had no doubt that Lenin had made a genuine effort to establish socialist principles in Russia.

On Christmas Day 1991, Gorbachev resigned and the next day the Soviet Union ceased to exist. A new organization, the Commonwealth of Independent States, was formed. Of course, the idealistic vision of pure socialism never materialized. It was unrealistic to expect that a welfare state like Denmark or Sweden could be built in a few years after seven decades of lawless gang rule. Gorbachev probably didn't fully realize this. He trusted advisers such as Grigory Yavlinsky, the economist and future leader of the Yabloko party, and Anatoly Chernyaev, himself an advocate of socialism with a human face. Alexander Yakovlev, his another aide, perhaps more perceptive, disagreed with Gorbachev, which resulted in endless arguments between them[27].

Boris Yeltsin, Gorbachev's successor, was probably more clear-sighted. He relied on the guidance of Yegor Gaidar and Anatoly Chubais as his main advisers. These economists had also studied Marx extensively and were deeply convinced that Russia should move as far away from his theories as possible. For them, the market was essential, and they were sure that once the market economy was in place, it wouldn't take long for the country to become prosperous.

Both Gorbachev and Yeltsin shared a belief in democracy and thought that combined with market principles it would improve the overall situation. Although Boris Yeltsin lacked knowledge of economics and the theory of 'scientific socialism', he respected and trusted his young advisers who had connections with colleagues in the Western world. He agreed to a series of drastic experimental reforms aimed at establishing a market economy.

In the USSR, as you know, everything was considered state property, although, as I have pointed out before, the state was effectively controlled by a small group of individuals. Yeltsin, following the recommendations of his advisers, decided to run a programme of privatization, returning to private ownership the assets that had been confiscated from millions of citizens sixty years earlier. This was his first major and consequential mistake. Neither Yeltsin nor Gorbachev before him realized that

26　Vladislav Zubok. *Zhivago's Children: The Last Russian Intelligentsia* (London: Harvard University Press, 2009); *The Idea of Russia. The Life and The Work of Dmitry Likhachev* (London: I. B.Tauris, 2016).

27　Анатолий С. Черняев, *Совместный исход. Дневник двух эпох. 1972–1991* (Москва: РОССПЭН, 2010); Александр Н. Яковлев, *Сумерки России* (Москва: Материк, 2003); Richard Pipes, *Alexander Yakovlev: The Man Whose Ideas Delivered Russia from Communism* (DeKalb: Northern Illinois University Press, 2015); Vladislav Zubok, *Collapse. The Fall of the Soviet Union* (London: Yale University Press, 2021).

the state had acquired its property illegally and that it should have been returned to the rightful successors of many ordinary people, the 'small people' as Churchill called them in his conversation with Stalin.

Nobody cared. Instead of identifying the rightful owners, land and other valuable resources were distributed among those who were closest to the 'higher powers' by those who had the authority, above all Yeltsin himself. Within a span of just two years, from 1992 to 1994, almost all of the country's assets – and Russia is a wealthy nation with abundant mining sites, significant oil production, vast forests, and extensive agricultural lands – ended up in the hands of a tiny group of individuals.

Only about one, maybe two percent of the population got all the income-generating property. A handful of people became instant millionaires. They didn't have exceptional economic skills, nor were they industrialists like Henry Ford. Their extraordinary success was simply related to their proximity to the centres of power. The problem is that the majority did not understand that they had been robbed again. Almost no one realized in 1991–1992 that they were actually owners of some property. Ironically, this time the beneficiaries of the transformations didn't understand that they were in fact robbers.

The situation in Russia was very different from that in Czechoslovakia, for example. In Czechoslovakia, almost everyone remembered that their parents, and perhaps even themselves if they belonged to an older generation, had owned something valuable – be it a piece of land, a house, a small or even a large factory. In Russia, by contrast, almost everyone had forgotten their lost property. This collective amnesia could be attributed to seven decades of communist propaganda, which had profoundly changed people's mindset and consciousness. In communist Russia, owning property was seen as something inherently negative, while having nothing was seen as a virtue. It is a paradox, but propaganda effectively hammered such distorted ideas into people's heads, while the country's leaders enjoyed a privileged life. Ordinary citizens didn't think of demanding the return of their families' stolen assets. Raising the issue was considered not only politically criminal, but morally reprehensible. Bolshevik propaganda machine constantly repeated that ordinary people were the masters of their country, and in some inexplicable way the population believed it. 'A man is the master of his vast motherland,' was a line from a popular song from Stalin's time. Thus, the Bolsheviks succeeded in convincing the majority of the moral superiority of collective ownership.

After the collapse of the Soviet Union in 1991, people found themselves even poorer than during the years of the communist regime. They looked back on those years with regret, because they remembered some social guarantees that really existed. Of course, they did not exist because the communists were driven by love for their countrymen, but because in any society it is necessary to provide basic services to the population, to maintain a strong army, to have a functioning industry, etc. Even slaves need some medical care so that they merciless exploitation could continue.

The return of lost property was not the main concern of the population. Rather, people wanted to regain social guarantees and were nostalgic for the well-structured communist past. Many believed that life in the USSR had been much better and safer, as there was strong social protection, so they did not have to worry about their future. They also witnessed a strange phenomenon: certain individuals around them became extraordinarily rich, while the majority continued to struggle in poverty.

Property rights were not the only issue; building a democratic society was also a challenge. With an unequal distribution of wealth, it was difficult for democratic principles to take root. In a truly people-ruled state, political parties would have sprung up immediately, arguing that public institutions were flawed, and that property had fallen into the wrong hands. These parties would have called for a return to a more equitable form of governance and offered various ways of improving the situation.

Indeed, a similar political conflict was brewing in Russia in 1993 and early 1994, leading to unrest and even an attempted coup d'état in October 1993. The Communists wanted a return to collective ownership and the Soviet past. Gregory Yavlinsky and his Yabloko party had a different approach: they proposed distributing almost everything equally among all the citizens of Russia, an idea that would have been both impractical and illegal. Curiously, very few people mentioned the need for property restitution, a path that had been followed almost everywhere in Eastern Europe, from Estonia to Albania, and, of course, in the Czech Republic. The Czech Republic is in fact one of the best examples of decommunization, as recognized by the European Commission.

Building a democracy when almost all citizens condemn the ownership of large properties is a formidable challenge in itself. The announced privatization process became popularly known as 'grab-itisation'. Even those who enriched themselves in the blink of an eye often realized that not everything was right. Gaidar, quite in the spirit of Marx, had to explain publicly that the first million is almost always earned illegally. But the people did not agree and demanded the restoration of an imaginary system in which everyone was poor but equal, so familiar to them from a bizarre mixture of endless empowering propaganda and personal experience of constant deprivation. The result of such aspirations could only be a new dictatorship, with a communist veneer of proclaimed equality, or the rule of the newly rich... Boris Yeltsin, persuaded by his entourage, chose the latter, while Gennady Zyuganov's 'communists' called for a return to Lenin's and, more often, Stalin's way of governance. It is worth noting that during the 1990s, pro-market advocates in Yeltsin's circle often expressed admiration for the Chilean dictator Augusto Pinochet. Pinochet came to power in 1973 after overthrowing the left-wing, USSR-aligned administration of Salvatore Allende, and ruled Chile with his 'iron hand' in an authoritarian and undemocratic manner until 1990.

Deep inequality thus made democracy unattainable in Russia in the early years of independence. As a result, the 1996 presidential elections, the first since the collapse of the Soviet Union, were marred by numerous forgeries and illegal manipulations. It became clear that democracy in Russia had come to an end.

I believe that restitution of property rights and the return to the rule of law is a normal process. For example, if robbers have taken away your possessions, they should rightfully be returned to you once the thieves are arrested. It would be very strange indeed if someone seized the stolen assets and claimed them as their own, forgetting about your rights. But that is exactly what happened in Russia in the 1990s.

The problem was compounded by the fact that few remembered that their families had once owned something. This was also the result of seven decades of Communist propaganda.

As a result, those who acquired property in Russia were not usually industrious and creative people. Instead, they had close ties to the former political establishment, particularly the KGB and the Communist Party leadership. Some of them were outright criminals. For example, the prominent politicians in Russia today, General Patrushev, General Bortnikov, General Sergei Ivanov and Sergei Naryshkin and others, have all become multimillionaires. Before the collapse of the Soviet Union, each of them held the rank of KGB general.

Yevgeny Prigozhin, another well-known figure, came from a very different background. In 1979, at the age of 18, he faced serious criminal charges and was sentenced to twelve years in prison. As a result, he spent his youth, from eighteen to thirty, behind bars until he was finally released in 1990 under an amnesty programme. After his release, Prigozhin became a businessman, and a well-known figure in Putin's entourage.

As you can see, this group of people, most of whom were former leaders of the Communist Party of the Soviet Union or high-ranking officials in the KGB, retained effective control over all of Russia's resources even after 1991. They got all of the country's assets, while the majority of the population was struggling in poverty and had to rely on their monthly salary to survive. Before the Bolshevik coup, up to 87–88% of Russians were private owners, who used their assets as a primary source of income. Russia had a higher percentage of such people than other European countries, largely due to the fact that many peasants had got land following the reforms of 1861.

However, the situation changed drastically after 1991. The core problem, and I'd like to emphasize this again, is that this small percentage of property owners is still largely made up of the descendants of the former Communist and KGB elite, as well as individuals associated with criminal groups whom the Bolsheviks considered 'socially close'. 'Today's authoritarian regime [...] is a logical result of privatization, a programme that was formulated, in part, by US advisers. [...] Privatization created a *sui generis* despotism, perhaps more entrenched than China's.' – Christopher Monday quite rightly pointed it out five years before Putin's current war of aggression against Ukraine[28].

In any country trying to break free from its dark past, property restitution is inevitably followed by lustration. The term itself comes from the Latin 'lustratio', meaning purification before a sacred ritual. This involves holding those who were part of the communist regime accountable, ensuring that they face legal consequences if they committed personal crimes, or barring them from any political activity because of their previous involvement with an illegal and criminal gang. Most countries in Eastern Europe softly implemented some form of it. However, in Russia and all the other former Soviet republics, with the exception of the Baltic states, nothing of the sort happened. Russian society was not purified. After seventy years of rule by a brutal band of robbers, the task of restoring democracy and justice was akin to a sacred endeavour. But it was undertaken by those who were themselves entangled in lies, covered in blood and morally corrupt. In Belarus, Ukraine, Kazakhstan and Uzbekistan, former Communist and KGB leaders and members of the Komsomol (Young Communist League) re-emerged as politicians, businessmen and formed the new elite. They didn't even bother to wash their hands first. The result was predictable[29].

The absence of both property restitution and lustration led to regimes that were only superficially democratic and market-oriented, paying only lip service to human values and freedoms. A closer look reveals that the same people who were part of the previous ruling class, or their children, continued to control all resources. In essence, nothing changed, and this lack of meaningful change prevented the emergence of true democracy in Russia and other former Soviet countries, including Ukraine.

There were, of course, some differences. Armenia and Ukraine were ruled by oligarchs, and Kazakhstan, Uzbekistan, Russia and Belarus adopted an authoritarian, almost monarchical form of government with one leader at the helm, but the core principle remained the unshaken. The previous elite, either personally or through their descendants, continued to dominate the post-Soviet space. There may have been some new faces in positions of power, but the basic structure and influence of the preceding regime were intact.

Ordinary people didn't engage in politics. How could they? Lack of resources makes it extremely difficult. It is only during a revolution that those without any possessions have a chance to become part of a political process. In the normal course of events, having some form of property is not only a safety net, but a prerequisite for feeling like a real citizen, a master of one's own country.

---

28   Christopher Monday, „Privatization to putinization: The genesis of Russia's hobbled oligarchy," *Communist and Post-Communist Studies*, Vol. 50 (2017): p. 303; 313.

29   Nikolai Bobrinsky, Natalia Kolyagina, Evgenia Lezina and Svetlana Shuranova. „The Russian Experience." In Natálie Maráková and Pavel Žáček (eds.). *Memory of Nations. Democratic Transition Guide [Experience of Selected Countries]* (Praha: CEVRO, z.s., 2017).

This becomes clear when we compare the Russian Revolution of 1917 with the French Revolution of 1789. In France, politicians still talk about the republican values of liberté, égalité and fraternité. This is no accident. Feudal dues were abolished during the French Revolution on August 4, 1789, and on July 17, 1792, ownership of land was granted to those who actually cultivated it, i.e. private tenants. It remains in the hands of their descendants to this day, as long as they have not sold it. After the restoration of the monarchy in 1815 under King Louis XVIII, the former landlords were compensated with one million gold francs, but the land was not taken back from the peasants. Property rights were respected. This explains why the country's core values of liberty, equality and fraternity still ring true today.

This was not the case in Russia, where events took a very different course. The Bolsheviks confiscated all land and outlawed private property. But after the collapse of the Soviet Union, no compensation was paid, and no restitution occurred. Instead, the former gangster elite remained in power, using the facade of democracy, market economy and civil rights as a mystification to hide their true identity. They continued to live essentially as they had, but now with much more openness because the Western world accepted them. There were no objections to former KGB bosses, apparatchiks like Boris Yeltsin himself, who used to be a member of the Central Committee of the Communist Party. They were welcomed as democratic leaders of newly independent states such as Russia, Kazakhstan, Belarus and Ukraine. The West seemed to turn a blind eye to the stark contrast between these countries and those that embraced genuine democratic reform, refusing to acknowledge that Belarus was different from the Czech Republic or that Kazakhstan was not like Romania.

In Russia and Belarus, the new rulers were so confident of their strength that they didn't even change the national symbols. Monuments to Lenin can still be seen in many towns and villages there. Portraits of Dzerzhinsky, a cruel and bloodthirsty tyrant, head of the NKVD, the Cheka, still hang in KGB buildings. In Kazakhstan, Uzbekistan, Azerbaijan and Armenia, Bolshevik lords have been replaced by statues of national leaders from the national pantheons.

The names of various streets and cities throughout Russia also bear the mark of the Bolshevik legacy. Some were renamed in the early years of independence, when the country was still hesitating about which direction to take. Leningrad, for example, became St Petersburg again, but the surrounding region is still called Leningradsky. The capital of the Urals was formerly known as Sverdlovsk, named after Yakov Sverdlov, who orchestrated the execution of Emperor Nicholas II. It has regained its original name, Yekaterinburg, but the region is still referred to as Sverdlovsky.

Many other places retain their Communist-era names. The old Russian city of Simbirsk is still called Ulyanovsk (Ulyanov was Lenin's real family name). There are many other examples of the continuing impact of the Communist regime, even many years after the collapse of the Soviet Union. The Bolshevik legacy is still present in the collective memory.

When Putin came to power, he further strengthened the symbolic links with the criminal communist past. He reintroduced the Soviet anthem, which had been abandoned under Yeltsin, and erected a commemorative plaque in honour of Andropov. Yuri Andropov, head of the KGB from 1967 to 1982, was known for his cruelty and relentless persecution of the anti-communist opposition. He even didn't hesitate to use medical and psychiatric wards as a method of punishment.

His commemorative plaque was removed in 1991, but Putin reinstalled it on the KGB headquarters, underlining the continuity of the secret police. We have been observing this pattern of gradual reconstruction of the Bolshevik past for many years. There is much talk now that the city of Tsaritsyn, now Volgograd, may soon revert to its Communist name of Stalingrad – a reference to the infamous Stalin. For nearly a year, there have been intense battles around the city in Donbass, which Ukrainians refer to by its historical name – Bakhmut. Russian official media call it Artemovsk, a name given to the city in 1924 in honour of the Bolshevik Fyodor Sergeyev's party alias, 'Artem.'

Let's not be fooled, there is no return to communist ideology, there has never been any. These are just symbols of criminal rule.

Another crucial aspect to consider is the legal framework that exists in Russia today. After the collapse of the USSR, not a single pre-communist law was reinstated. The Russian Empire used to have a large body of laws that were in line with the country's new democratic aspirations. For example, it had well-developed provisions on private property, which was considered almost sacred. Although the 1993 Constitution stipulated that all laws that had existed in Russia in the past and did not contradict its principles should remain in force, this clause was applied only to Soviet-era legal texts, many of which are still valid today. In practice, this means that Soviet laws, including those on property confiscation, continue to apply until a new bill replaces them. The legal system is still heavily influenced by the totalitarian past.

It is not surprising that the Russian Federation, as the most powerful successor of the Bolshevik state, has once again adopted an aggressive foreign policy and unleashed a full-fledged war against its neighbour. As we have shown in previous lectures, the criminal regime had no concern for the people's welfare, equality or democracy. Instead, its goal was to expand the territory and influence of the state, as seen in its pursuit of a global communist empire before World War II.

Czechoslovakia was one of the first victims of their aggression, when Stalin decided to annex Subcarpathian Rus in 1945, and then when the Soviet army occupied the whole country in 1968. However, these actions are not rooted in the aspirations of the Russian people, but in the ambitions of the gangster elite in power. The Russian people are also subjected to a powerful propaganda machine that influences their beliefs and actions, spreading false ideas that bring nothing but sorrow and suffering.

For example, the state is constantly trying to persuade the population that the glory of Russia will somehow compensate for the deprivations of real life. Many ordinary Russians continue to live in dire economic conditions. And they are the main target of such intensive propaganda. Let's not forget that their desire for a 'strong and great Russia' is in fact not their own. It has been taught to them by their elite, the same gangsters that have maintained their grip on Russia for many years.

Putin's thirst for power and dominance led him to launch a war against Ukraine in 2014, which turned into a full-scale invasion on 24 February 2022. Wars in Syria and Libya follow the same logic as he attempted to secure military bases and control resources in the eastern Mediterranean.

Putin and his inner circle have been harbouring these expansionist dreams for some time. I remember them talking about such aspirations as early as 2008–2010. It is obvious that these aggressive and bloody schemes do not benefit ordinary people.

In 2014, Angela Merkel said that Putin had lost touch with reality. He has. But he has never lost touch with the Soviet past. A former high-ranking KGB officer, he is still infatuated with the crazy ideas of the Bolsheviks.

The terrible war between Russia and Ukraine has been raging for 18 months. Countless lives have been lost and many people have been made homeless. This conflict has brought immense suffering and devastation to the people of Ukraine, as well as grief and sorrow to many Russians. Over a million Russians have been forced to leave their country because they do not support the aggression. Many of them do not understand the reasons behind Putin's actions.

The answer lies, as you already know, in the criminal principles by which Russia has been governed since 1917. Putin, driven by the same aggressive mentality as his predecessors, saw an opportunity to extend his influence. He thought he was strong enough. But his calculation turned out to be a serious mistake. The war did not go as planned and did not bring him the desired results.

The continued resistance and resilience of the Ukrainian people, coupled with international pressure and sanctions, have made the war increasingly costly and unsuccessful for Putin. This series of missteps has put the Putin regime on shaky ground, and we may soon see a decline in his power.

What will the future look like? This is not a purely academic question. It's important to understand the history that has brought us to the present situation, but it's up to politicians, not historians, to answer it. As the liberation of Ukraine becomes a reality, negotiations will be necessary between Moscow, Kyiv and Europe. Is it possible to negotiate with bandits? I think not. Replacing Putin with Patrushev or Prigozhin won't bring any meaningful change. We need a radical overhaul of the regime, not just a name swap.

Even if Putin is replaced by someone who appears more liberal but shares the same ideology and continues the legacy of the last 100 years, nothing substantial will change. We must not fall for the illusion of pseudo-democracy, pseudo-market practices or pseudo-liberal posturing in international affairs.

If we – and I mean all ordinary Russians, all people of the free world from Japan to the EU and the US – are really determined to put an end to this inhuman system, there are a few things we need to understand. We must not be deceived about the nature of the Russian policy-makers. Then we must recognize that entering into any kind of agreement with this regime before lustration takes place is not a viable option. Lustration used to be an unresolved internal issue for Russia. But now that Russia has become an aggressor, and the European Parliament has even declared it a supporter of terrorism, the problem has taken on an international dimension. Its importance and the prospects for its implementation in Russia after Putin are analysed in detail in a paper by Nikolai Bobrinsky and Stanislav Dmitrievsky, which was published in Russian just before the outbreak of a full-scale war with Ukraine[30].

Other countries should be made absolutely clear: no discussions or negotiations until there is real lustration and meaningful changes in Russia. Such a message can only come from the international community, not from the Russian people, who live under a constant torrent of government propaganda.

Russia can only be represented in negotiations by those who are not part of the criminal gang in power. There should be no former KGB strongmen like Patrushev and Bortnikov, nor members of Putin's inner circle like Prigozhin and Kadyrov. A new Russian regime should be free of such individuals.

Real democracy, not an imitation of it, must be an absolute prerequisite for any engagement with Russia. Russian leaders, from Lenin onwards, have excelled in keeping up democratic appearances, but we should not play this game. There was a brief period of democracy under Gorbachev, when there were real elections, that's all. Yeltsin was the only democratically elected president of Russia in June 1991, just before the collapse of the USSR.

Without a real commitment to democracy, Russia cannot be seen as a side with which the free world can negotiate. We cannot compromise on this. Only when Russia fully embraces and genuinely implements democratic principles can the international community reconsider sanctions and welcome Russia back into the fold of civilized nations.

It is important to understand the process of democratization in post-communist societies. There is a significant difference between the post-communist world and the post-Nazi world, because the Nazis were not against private property, they didn't confiscate it. Consequently, the issue of property restitution was not present in Germany

---

30   Николай Бобринский и Станислав Дмитриевский, *Между местью и забвением: концепция переходного правосудия для России: аналитический доклад* (Москва: Институт права и публичной политики, 2020). (English translation to be published in 2023). Available at trjustice.ilpp.ru

after World War II, but it became an absolute necessity for the countries recovering from communism.

Property restitution is necessary. Without it, the road to democracy is blocked and the only possible form of government is some sort of dictatorship – it doesn't matter what kind – left or right, Stalin's or Pinochet's. Without democracy, there won't be a predictable and reliable Russia. Therefore, property restitution is essential for the normalization of relations with our country and for lasting peace in this part of the world.

Then there is the problem of symbols. Monuments to Bolshevik leaders, streets and cities named after terrible murderers, testify to an unwillingness to break with the dark past and violent history. We can't ignore them.

Every country chooses symbols that reflect its values. If a nation celebrates and glorifies criminals, its politics will undoubtedly be tainted by dubious ideologies. To use an analogy, I think it would be fair to say that a monument to a Nazi leader would be unthinkable in Germany today.

The situation in Russia is no different. If, after the war, Russia seeks to restore normal relations with the world, the international community should respond with caution. The presence of Lenin's unburied body in the heart of Russia, right on Red Square, along with numerous monuments glorifying other notorious Bolsheviks, be they Dzerzhinsky, Kirov, Sverdlov or Stalin, is a loud message about the government's true priorities. Changing them should be one of the first acts of the new leadership, otherwise it won't have any credibility.

Reversing the cultural paradigm from celebrating Lenin and Dzerzhinsky to honouring the real victims of the Bolshevik regime and those who fought with it is not a secondary matter; it is crucial and central to any reconciliation and progress. Among those who deserve recognition are the Czech and Slovak legionnaires who fought courageously against the communists in 1918–1920, even if their efforts seemed futile at the time.

Next, Russia should be demilitarized. While changing national symbols and embarking on political reforms towards democracy are laudable actions, it would be difficult to fully guarantee that Russia's formidable nuclear capabilities won't be misused if power were to fall back into the hands of those closely associated with its dark past.

If we recall the scenario of post-Nazi Germany after World War II, we know that it took more than a decade before the Bundeswehr was allowed to operate independently in 1956. Even then, it continued to function only under NATO control. It was not until 1991 that the Bundeswehr achieved full autonomy. A similar approach may be necessary for Russia if it is to move forward and regain international trust after its reprehensible aggression. Giving up the full independence of its armed forces and placing them under NATO control, at least temporarily, could prove essential.

Decartelization is another important measure, as companies such as Rosneft, Gazprom, Severstal and Norilsknikel are in fact quasi-private entities operating under state supervision. Take the case of Mikhail Khodorkovsky, who was sentenced to ten years in prison in the early 2000s for trying to sell his oil company Yukos to British Petroleum without Putin's approval. As a result, Yukos was placed under the control of people appointed by Putin, and its owner, who wanted to act independently, found himself behind bars. Other high-income companies operate under similar conditions.

In the effort to consolidate democracy, it will be crucial to encourage independent economic ventures in various sectors, including gas, oil, metals and timber. I'm not an economist myself, but I firmly believe that decartelization is an essential step for post-Putin Russia. The same approach worked in Germany after the end of the Nazi regime, and it played a crucial role in Germany's reintegration into the community of democratic nations.

Finally, it is important to combat government propaganda. The international community must send a clear message to Russia: calls for the restoration of an empire, idealization of Communist leaders and denial of the horrific repression of the Bolshevik era are unacceptable. If they continue, it will be impossible to improve relations with Russia. Just as Germany strictly prohibits the glorification of Nazism, the display of Nazi symbols and the veneration of Nazi leaders, Russia should criminalize the propagation and justification of criminal Bolshevism and its modern manifestation in the form of Putinism.

Perhaps all these measures should have been implemented in 1992 or at the end of 1991. Unfortunately, no one in the West seriously considered this, nor did Russia or the other post-Bolshevik states (with the exception of Estonia, Latvia and Lithuania). Therefore, the failure to address the internal challenges over the course of three decades has had dire consequences, culminating in the devastating war in Europe.

Russia will undoubtedly continue to exist in one form or another, and the nearly 120 million native speakers of the Russian language won't disappear. However, the pressing concern for the whole world, especially Europe and the democratic regions of Asia, is how to deal with Russia's future. Should we try to transform it into a democratic, normal state? After all, we have a success story of s in West Germany, Italy, Austria and Japan after the World War II. Or should we leave it as it is?

The Treaty of Versailles changed Germany's borders. The country lost its colonies, had to pay reparations and faced military restrictions. But Germany was essentially left to its own devices. Fifteen years later, Hitler came to power and the world was plunged into a series of catastrophic events that led to another world war. The cost was enormous – more than 80 million deaths, the Holocaust, material and moral devastation across Europe, the Far East, North Africa, Oceania and Indochina.

For both Europeans and Russians who believe in democratic ideals, repeating the mistakes of the past, such as those made at Versailles, is simply unthinkable. Our responsibility is to bring about Russia's internal transformation, not just to restore its facade. It's our shared task–yours, mine, the duty of all the people of the world who yearn to live in peace. It is imperative to transform Russia into a normal state, and to do this we must acknowledge its past and draw on the lessons of denazification. In this endeavour, history transcends academic rooms and becomes the true teacher of life, helping us to shape the future of the earth for the benefit of all.

Bibliography

Sources in Russian

Андреев, Е.М., Л.Е.Дарский и Т.Л. Харькова. *Население Советского Союза: 1922–1991.* Москва: Наука, 1993.

Арцыбашев, Михаил П. *Показания по делу Конради. Красный террор в Москве.* Москва: Айрис Пресс, 2010.

Бобринский, Николай; Дмитриевский, Станислав. *Между местью и забвением: концепция переходного правосудия для России: аналитический доклад.* Москва: Институт права и публичной политики, 2020. Available at https://trjustice.ilpp.ru/ [08-09-2023].

Жиромская, В.Б. и Поляков, Ю.А. (Сост.). *Всесоюзная перепись населения. 1937. Общие итоги. Сборник документов и материалов.* Москва: РОССПЭН, 2007.

Зубов, Андрей (ed.). *История России. XX век.* Москва, 2016.

Зубов, Андрей. „Это уже было.“ *Ведомости* (March 2014). Available at https://www.vedomosti.ru/opinion/articles/2014/03/01/andrej-zubov-eto-uzhe-bylo [08-09-2023]

Зубов, Андрей. "Кто хотел войны в 1914 г. и стал ли миром Версальский мир. Опыт сравнения с сегодняшним днем," *Новая газета* (September 2014). Available at https://novayagazeta.ru/articles/2014/09/13/61131-professor-andrey-zubov-prichiny-i-posledstviya-pervoy-mirovoy voyny [08-09-2023]

Зубов, Андрей. „Европа и мир: Рубежи земли и предназначение цивилизаций.“ *Континент* (Москва-Paris), no 83 (1995).

Кузнецов, Виктор И. (ed.). *Тайна Октябрьского переворота: Ленин и немецко-большевистский заговор. Документы, статьи, воспоминания.* Санкт-Петербург: Алетейя, 2001.

Маклаков, Василий А. *Власть и общество на закате старой России. Воспоминания современника.* Москва: Новое литературное обозрение, 2023.

Миро́нов, Бори́с Н. *Социальная история России*. Санкт-Петербург: Дмитрий Буланин, 2000.

Найшуль, В. А. *Другая жизнь*. Москва: самиздат, 1985.

Померанц, Григорий. *Записки гадкого утенка [Notes of an Ugly Duckling]*. Москва: Московский рабочий, 1998.

РГАСПИ, Ф17., Оп.84, Д.111. Л.80б-9.

РГАСПИ, Ф558., Оп.1, Д.766. Л.18-19.

Черняев, Анатолий С. *Совместный исход. Дневник двух эпох. 1972–1991*. Москва: РОССПЭН, 2010.

Яковлев, Александр Н. *Сумерки России*. Москва: Материк, 2003.

Sources in other languages

Baumgart, Winfried. *Deutsche Ostpolitik 1918. Von Brest-Litowsk bis Zum Ende des Ersten Weltkrieges*. Munich: R. Oldenbourg Verlag. 1966.

Bobrinsky, Nikolai; Kolyagina, Natalia; Lezina, Evgenia; Shuranova, Svetlana. „The Russian Experience." In Maráková, Natálie and Pavel Žáček (eds.). *Memory of Nations. Democratic Transition Guide [Experience of Selected Countries]*. Praha: CEVRO, z.s., 2017.

Churchill, Winston. *The Second World War: Volume IV*. Boston: Houghton, Mifflin Company, 1950.

Frei, Norbert. *Der Führerstaat. Nationalsozialistische Herrschaft 1933–1945*. Munich: dtv, 1987. Translated into English as *National Socialist Rule in Germany: The Führer State 1933–1945*. Translated by Simon B. Steyne. Oxford, Cambridge: Blackwell Publishers 1993.

Fukuyama, Francis. "The End of History?" *The National Interest*, no. 16 (Summer 1989).

Fukuyama, Francis. *The End of History and the Last Man*. New York: Free Press, 1992.

Hosking, Geoffrey. Russian History. A Very Short Introduction. London: Oxford University Press, 2012.

Lampe, John R. *Yugoslavia as History: Twice There Was a Country*. New York: Cambridge University Press, 2000.

Malia, Martin. *Comprendre la révolution russe*. Paris: Éditions du Seuil, 1980.

Monday, Christopher. „Privatization to putinization: The genesis of Russia's hobbled oligarchy," *Communist and Post-Communist Studies*, Vol. 50 (2017): pp. 303–317.

Obolensky, Dimitri. *The Byzantine Commonwealth: Eastern Europe, 500-1453*. London: Cardinal, 1971.

Pipes, Richard. *Alexander Yakovlev: The Man Whose Ideas Delivered Russia from Communism*. DeKalb: Northern Illinois University Press, 2015.

Pipes, Richard. *Russia Under the Bolshevik Regime: 1919–1924*. New York: Alfred A. Knopf, 1993.

Pipes, Richard. *The Russian Revolution*. New York: Alfred A. Knopf, 1990.

Radkey, Oliver H. *Russia goes to the polls: the election to the all-Russian Constituent Assembly, 1917*. Ithaca: Cornell University Press, 1989.

Toynbee, Arnold J. *A Study of History*. London: Oxford University Press, 1987. Reissue, abridged by D. C. Somervell.

Vernadsky, George. *Lenin: Red Dictator*. New Haven: Yale university Press, 1931.

Zeman, Zbyněk A. B. (ed.). *Germany and the Revolution in Russia 1915–1918. Documents from the Archives of the German Foreign Ministry*. London: Oxford University Press, 1958.

Zubok, Vladislav. *Collapse. The Fall of the Soviet Union*. London: Yale University Press, 2021.

Zubok, Vladislav. *The Idea of Russia. The Life and The Work of Dmitry Likhachev*. London: I. B. Tauris, 2016.

Zubok, Vladislav. *Zhivago's Children: The Last Russian Intelligentsia*. London: Harvard University Press, 2009.

U

V

W

Y

Z

The Russian Catastrophe

and Chances to Overcome It

Andrey Borisovich Zubov

Language assistance and proofreading by Chris Rance and Anton Klevansky
Cover photo by Daniil Zubov
Preface by Jiří Hanuš
Edited by Martina Dvořáková
Layout and typesetting by Pavel Křepela
Printed by Tiskárny Havlíčkův Brod, a.s., Husova 1881, Havlíčkův Brod
Published by Masaryk University in 2023
First edition

ISBN 978-80-280-0384-5
ISBN 978-80-280-0385-2 (online ; pdf)
www.press.muni.cz